MW01143851

ROBERT COWAN

LIVING
A
BIBLICAL
CULTURE

in a darkening world

Thoughts along the Path

"Scripture taken from the NEW AMERICAN STANDARD BIBLE, © 1960, 1962, 1963, 1968, 1971, 1972, 1973, 1975, 1977, by The Lockman Foundation. Used by permission."

Back Cover photograph: Robert M. Cowan
Cover design: Robert M. Cowan

ISBN: 978-1-68222-950-7

Printed in the United States of America

This book is dedicated to

my Heavenly family,
the Father, Son and Holy Spirit;

and to my earthly family,
Debi, David, Emily and Matthew,

all for whom I have tried to
live a biblical culture
in a darkening world.

This book is intended
for the generation of
'twenty something's'
who were kids
when I pastored them;

but I hope it proves helpful
to all who read it
with 'eyes to see and ears to hear.'

Contents

Living a Biblical Culture in a darkening world

It was in the early morning hours of January 21st, 1972 that I fell completely in love with Jesus! At that moment in time He began to emerge as my best friend, the literal and spiritual Saviour of my soul and Lord of my life. Today I look back with deep and utter gratitude for every activity God has graciously allowed me to be a part of, with Jesus as 'my Way, my Truth and the supreme love of my Life' (John 14:6a). His incomparably powerful Spirit has been my faithful Guide and Counsellor all the way!

Most of my life I have served smaller congregations as a pastor/teacher. I have not been a sought after conference speaker, or a particularly brilliant communicator. I have not led a highly sinless life, or sense that I have 'arrived' in any fashion... but I have doggedly followed the 'narrow path' (Matthew 7:14) and tried to live a biblical lifestyle wherever Jesus has taken me.

In this book I would like to simply and humbly share some of the thoughts that have come to me through the years, which have both solidified a biblical framework for me, and helped me live out a biblical culture in my own life's journey as a devoted child of God and passionate disciple of Jesus Christ.

INTRODUCTION

This is not meant to be a theological treatise, nor is it intended to be a scholarly analysis of biblical material. Rather, it is simply a collection of thoughts which have developed in my own mind and heart over the years, which I now have a desire to pass along to the *twenty something's* in what I consider to be 'darkening days'. The topic titles are given simply to provide some order and progression to these somewhat random thoughts. It is not my intention to give a comprehensive treatment of any of the subjects themselves.

I write now, not just because of the 'times' we are living in, but more due to the aging season of my life. The parts of these writings that refer to the 'darkening days' are my own limited personal observations of how I see God 'winding down' our world. For me, this gives rise to an accompanying urgency among believers to forgo the cultural norms of whatever society we live in and whatever cultural values we have become entangled with, in order to engender a more biblical culture at the very core of our soul!

My goal is to put to pen how God has helped me view the world in such a way as to remain an effective disciple of His for the spiritual benefit of others, in whatever cultures He has taken me. I do not ask you to agree with all my thoughts, but I sincerely hope and pray that some of them will inspire you to follow my example of living out a spiritually effective biblical culture in this darkening world!

There is an interesting passage of Scripture which reads,

"But the day of the Lord will come like a thief, in which the heavens will pass away with a roar and the elements will be destroyed with intense heat, and the earth and its works will be burned up. Since all these things are to be destroyed in this way, what sort of people ought you to be in holy conduct and godliness"   *2 Peter 3:10-11 (NASB)*

If I were to pursue this passage theologically I would quote the entire third chapter of 2 Peter, for it deserves a careful and contemplative study. But being introductory in these remarks, suffice it to say I believe we need to shed our culture in every way it distracts us from 'holy conduct and godliness'.

With my current ministry in Honduras, Central America, I find myself often urging people to 'stop being Honduran, to stop being Canadian, American, African or Italian', and to live as committed citizens of heaven, the culture of which is outlined in the Word of God. Now more than ever, as our world increasingly secularizes, we must not only distinguish between what is 'of the world' and what is 'of God', but choose to give our primary, in fact our full allegiance to the activity of God in this world. This means living carefully by the principles laid out in the Scriptures, rather than by the circumstances of life within the indoctrinated framework of a human culture. It means dying to sin by denying yourself daily and living for Christ (Romans 6:11; Mark 8:34; 1 Peter 2:24).

I do not by any means speak from a lofty place, for sinfulness is a daily struggle, and the Divine hand of the Trinity is my only means of achieving true victory each day. I thank Jesus so deeply for 'never leaving or forsaking me' (Hebrews 13:5). It is only by His grace that any of us stand, for 'no man can come to Jesus unless the Father draws him' (John 6:44).

It is my hope that a thoughtful and practical reading of this material will stimulate some to "love and good deeds" (Hebrews 10:24b), and others to a complete transformation of thinking (Romans 12:2) and living (Romans 14:8), as God continues to draw this present world to a close.

TESTIMONY

Let me begin by outlining my own journey toward living a biblical lifestyle.

I believe I was called and chosen by God (2 Peter 1:10) to serve His Kingdom. At the height of the *'Jesus Movement'* of the '70s, I was among many freshly elected into His glorious Kingdom to become a new generation of disciple making leaders, called into service for my risen Saviour, Jesus Christ. God had been preparing me through my upbringing, through my inner consciousness of the depraved lifestyle I was drifting into, and through the very circumstances which brought about my abrupt and merciful salvation. He wooed me toward Himself and introduced me to His Son, Jesus, in the precise ways I needed to be.

My first encounter with Jesus was highly personal and intimate, and ultimately shaped the very course of my life. It became, and continues to be the passion of my life to please Him, and to infuse in all around me the opportunity to experience the depth, intimacy and powerful relationship available with God through His Son, Jesus Christ.

It was the winter of my fourteenth year and I was a rather pudgy youth making a poorly conceived attempt at being cool! Following in the footsteps of my well-known drug dealing cousin up north, I jumped headlong into all the destructive things a nerdy kid might do in a quest to impress the popular school crowd. But all it got me was to be jeered at, slammed into locker doors, made fun of, and generally treated as one with little or no value to the world around me.

Interestingly, one year later, these same 'A' grade teen students were secretly coming to me at the lunch table, relating their innermost problems and fears, and thankful for my listening ear and insightful advice. What happened to produce such a significant change in such a short period of time? Well, I met and fell in love with Jesus, Son of the Living God, Creator and Sustainer of the universe and beyond!

Backdrop

My one older sister and I grew up in a morally upright Canadian middle class family. My mother worked as a teacher and my father as an office manager. My father taught me how things worked, and how to build and construct things. My mother showed me how to make things and how to solve problems.

Mom grew up a self-sufficient city girl, with a mother quite absorbed in her career, operating the first Canadian Conservatory of Music in Toronto, Canada. Dad grew up a country boy of pioneering parents, milking cows in the mornings before going to a one room school house. His mother gardened the land for food and tended to four rough and tumble sons, while his Dad shod horses and constructed cottages, boathouses and docks for very wealthy families in Muskoka, a famous lake district in Ontario.

The languages spoken in our home were *provision* and *instruction*. Love and relationship were not spoken of, at least not to me. My sister lived distanced from me, so I am honestly not sure how she was raised or how she related to my parents. She seemed happy enough for the most part.

I remember one time going to Cowan Lake (named after an Uncle killed in World War II) to be taught how to swim. My father set me on his broad naked back, walked out into the deeper water and began to swim around with me clinging to his neck. I remember that because I felt a rare warmth of love in that moment, both for him and from him.

My mother occasionally took me to the old Royal Alexandra Theatre downtown Toronto to see productions like 'The King and I' and 'The Sound of Music'. I remember holding her hand tightly as we descended the extremely steep staircase of the upper balcony, thinking what a wonder it was to have someone care enough to give me such opportunities!

When we visited my grandfather Cowan up in Muskoka, he would always be reading a big black Bible while awaiting our arrival. I knew it was important to him, but its contents were a mystery to me. One particular weekend he gave me one (he had several). It was the strangest thing having that book in my bedroom. For years it sat there, and somehow it seemed very special to me. It dropped off my shelf once and I thought something bad was going to happen to me. Another time I inadvertently set my homework on top of it. Realizing what I had done, I quickly removed it. This book seemed to speak to me of something, or 'Someone' very special, but I never did open it, except to read the genealogy of our family, my grandmother had written in the pages between the Testaments (whatever those were).

When I was still quite young, our family for some reason started attending a United Church in Oakville, the town in Ontario where I was raised. I enjoyed sitting in the balcony leaning against my Dad's arm. It was probably the closest I ever got to him. My Dad got involved in Saturday church projects, helping to landscape the yard and paint the building. After about a year he was walking out of the sanctuary one Sunday and the minister shook his hand and commented, "Hello, are you new here?" That was the last Sunday we ever attended church as a family.

When I was ten years old my parents decided my sister and I ought to get acquainted with the larger world, so we began to take a family trip each year, beginning with Canada and the USA, then farther afield to the Caribbean, Europe and, for me, Africa. By this time we had built our own family cottage in Muskoka and I felt very fortunate to have been presented with so much of this world to enjoy and explore.

But everything given me was of this world. The Bible or God was never mentioned to me, except for one memory that sticks in my mind.

We used to go to a neighbour's house on school mornings as my parents sped off to their career lives. This family for some reason started sending their two kids to a local Baptist Church. My sister got involved in the girl's club there, and one night as I lay in bed, I could hear my Mom helping her memorize the books of the Bible. From that single night of listening I could then recite every book in the Bible!

Soon after, this family's son convinced me to go to the boy's club, where I first heard some Bible verses, although I had no idea what they were about! Later on, my friend and I would occasionally go to the church service on Sunday and tease girls in the balcony. I have to admit that not once did I pay attention to the words coming from the stage!

Then one day something so simple, yet miraculous happened! I had my first personal encounter with the Living God! It was a crisp fall day and I was walking to school. Every day for me was filled with this world. I left a man-made home, walked on a man-made asphalt road to a man-made school, passing man-made signs, garbage cans and garage doors, smoking man-made cigarettes. But this day was different. All of a sudden I glanced into the sky and noticed EVERYTHING that was NOT made by man as if for the first time in my life; the colour sky blue, the wispy white clouds, the crescent moon in the quiet morning, then the lush green grass, the shapes and contours of the trees. It was at this moment I first believed there was a God, a Creator. In fact, I said right out loud, "There IS a God!" I continued on to school, butting out my cigarette and walking in with a new lightness to my step.

I will never forget that gift from God Himself! It was as though He had preordained every moment of my entire life leading up to that point, and then declared to the worshipping angels, "Ok! Watch this! I am about to pour out My blessed love into this foolish 15 year old boy and turn him into a discipler of nations!"

Shortly after this event, I agreed to attend a winter Retreat sponsored by a local Baptist Church, at a camp north of the city. I was excited because we would be driving there with a race car driver who loved to do 'donuts' along the way! My hope was to go out on the snowmobiles with my friend while the 'talks' were taking place. The first night was bitter cold outside. As I gazed over at the snow machines, some of the staff hopped on and took off up and over the hill. Because it was so cold, I went back inside and sat down on the floor where the speaker was talking. For the very first time I actually 'listened' to a message!

The guy began bragging about his best friend. He told us his friend was always there for him, never let him down, cared deeply about his life, and kept him company when he was lonely. On and on he went, and I was captivated! Deep down in my own lonely heart I longed for a friend like his. I had taken up smoking and drug use to 'fit in' with the popular crowd and get invited to the 'right' parties. So there I was, in the middle of grade eleven, with hair half way down my back, attempting to appear 'cool' and important... sitting on that piece of floor longing for a 'real' friend! Well, as the talk came to a close, the speaker declared, "... and the best thing of all about my friend is... He is also the Son of God!" What? I didn't know God had a Son? How did that happen? What?

I went home from that weekend full of questions, and full of hope! God had a Son who came to this earth and died to free me from my sins so I could be forgiven; so I could walk through life with true purpose and meaning and then end up in heaven? My mind was blown!

By the next Friday at two in the morning I could not even sleep. I took that old black Bible and went down the hall into the bathroom. There, seated on the 'throne' I said to God, "I am going to open this book and start to read. If You are really there and this is all true, then speak to me and tell me what to do." The Bible opened to Joshua 24. Now for those with Bible knowledge you realize that Joshua is filled with battles and somewhat obscure stories, but here is the first thing I read! I looked at the page and my eye landed on verse 14. It said,

"Now, therefore, fear the Lord and serve Him in sincerity and truth; and put away the gods which your fathers served beyond the River and in Egypt [I had no idea what that part meant, except that there were things I was supposed to put away from my life], and serve the Lord".

At this exact moment in my existence, all of creation, my being on this earth, and the purpose and meaning of life, everything consolidated and my world finally made complete sense! From that moment to the very moment I am writing this book, I have never looked back, never regretted my choice to follow Jesus, never second guessed the existence of God and never wanted a life without Jesus as my Saviour and Lord!

This is the backdrop of my life. God took me and made me into a discipler of nations, and to this day I still anticipate with joy each opportunity I have left to speak of Him and to involve myself in the things of His Kingdom that really matter to the people of this earth! I trust as you read through these personal thoughts you will be drawn closer to Him yourself, experience the wonder of knowing Him and surrender the rest of your life into His eternal purposes.

Beginnings

The next afternoon I phoned the secretary at the Baptist Church and said, "Could you get the minister to do one of those things where he asks people to come to the front, because I want to do that!" This was followed by quite a long pause, and then "Uh, ok." Well, he gave a call that Sunday night and I responded! As I walked to the front everything that had weighed down my life just fell off me, and I felt like I was almost floating. One of the men took me aside and shared some Scripture verses with me, to make sure I understand what I had just done; and since that transforming evening I have never looked back.

Shortly after, I was baptized, to demonstrate publicly my joyful new life commitment to God through the shed blood of His Son, by the power of the Spirit!

At this young age of fifteen, I was further blessed to become part of a mighty outpouring of the Holy Spirit upon a generation of followers, labeled by some as the "Jesus People". Larry Norman and Randy Stonehill were singing *Why don't you look into Jesus, He's got the answer!* and Keith Green was lamenting the failure of the established church to reach out, in his penetrating song *Asleep in the Light*. Chuck Smith was pioneering a church accepting of hippies and sinners, and teens like Paul and Stephen Bramer, mentored by godly parents, Doug and Vera, were hitchhiking to huge Jesus rallies around the country.

We each began to grow in our own faith, gathering in the Bramer's basement Fridays nights to share our new understanding of Scriptures! From that one little room emerged a generation of Christian workers and leaders who have set aflame thousands of disciples over these last couple of decades! We created songbooks with a hand-cranked Gestetner machine, wrote poems to Jesus, prayed our hearts out to God, sang for hours, even writing our own lyrics. We discussed every passage of Scripture we read as if no one had ever seen it before and our very lives depended upon understanding and obeying it. Many of the guys and some of the girls learned to play guitar in that room. Lesson one was a 'G' chord. Whenever a 'G' popped up over the lyrics in the songbook, we would strum a 'G' until another letter took over. Lesson two was a 'D' chord, then a 'C', followed by trying to jam all three fingers together to play an 'A'. Of course 'F' was simply impossible so we all faked it as best we could.

The privilege and significance of those times spent in the Bramer's basement becoming disciples of Jesus Christ cannot be measured. All the while Doug and Vera (Ma and Pa) Bramer stood by upstairs, ready and alert at any point to offer spiritual encouragement, not to mention pop and chips!!

I would venture to say that if you travel to almost any region of the globe today, you will find a discipling community that bears the imprint and impact of either a discipler from the Bramer basement or of someone who was discipled by one of them! Not only across North America, east to west, and north to south, but Central and South America, the Philippines, Hong Kong, Vietnam and Thailand, South and East Africa, Scotland and England, even in the cradle of civilization itself - Jerusalem and our precious Bethlehem Ephrata.

Be encouraged that when the Holy Spirit prompts just a few to become intimate with God through a real, living and a responsive love relationship with His Son Jesus, the 'King of all kings and Lord of all lords' (1 Timothy 6:15), there is no end to the ripple effect upon an entire generation.

I was privileged to attend a small (very open) Brethren Assembly in those first few years of my Christian experience. Early Sunday mornings before the regular service began, we would gather within a small square of chairs, four sections all facing a simply constructed table, housing the 'bread and a cup'. Listening to those men randomly stand and pray or share biblical thoughts, and then gathering the nerve to get up ourselves and somehow participate, took us to the heights of heaven and behind the veil to the Holy of Holies where God dwells, let me tell you!

A few years later, during the course of a year spent at Berklee College of Music in Boston, I attended a small Brethren Church on Sunday mornings. After service, one or another of the older men would inevitably invite me back to their home where they would feed me lunch and then uncover the depths of Scripture to me. Why me, I never quite grasped, but it served to further mentor me toward a biblical lifestyle that transcended any human culture around me. It paved the way for me to travel life on a quest for the narrow path "that leads to life" (Matthew 7:14).

I remember one significant day after a church service back in Canada, before heading off to Bible College in Toronto. One of the oldest men took me aside under the basement stairwell. He reminded me of where Jesus had said to His followers in Luke 10:39-42 that Mary was "listening to the Lord's word, seated at His feet", and then to her sister, "Martha, Martha, you are worried and bothered about so many things; but *only* a few things are necessary, really only one, for Mary has chosen the good part, which shall not be taken away from her." He said, "Bob, don't ever forget that Mark 10:39 is the only real Bible College that matters; seated at the feet of Jesus attentively listening to His every Word" (... and he was right!).

You see, even Jesus boiled all things important down to one concise, focus... reading and responding to His Word. There lies the blessed life, not all the things a human culture throws at us to cling to. Much time spent in the Word seeking an understanding of how to humbly respond to Him, brings about a culture of biblical living that far exceeds the pale distractions of this world and the crafty deceptions of the evil one. May you know the joy I experience daily by giving myself to His service!

CULTURE

The sheer beauty of living a biblical culture
is how effective it is for His Kingdom.

I believe the issue of *culture* is so paramount to attaining the biblical lifestyle of a disciple that I have chosen to make it the first topic of discussion.

My goal throughout this book is to demonstrate the value of actually and practically living a 'biblical culture' "in such a way that they may see your good works, and glorify your Father who is in heaven" (Matthew 5:16). There are ways to do this, and I would like the privilege of sharing some of the thoughts He has given me; ways to walk in your culture, yet live responsively by His Spirit, maintaining an eternal perspective. Some thoughts may seem so far removed from earthly views that you will have a difficult time digesting them. But this is what I sense He wants me to lay before you, the next generation of His potential disciples, in the midst of darkening days.

As early as Genesis 10 God spoke of nations, family groupings with specific languages, separated onto various parcels of land.

"From these the coastlands of the nations were separated into
their lands, every one according to his language, according to
their families, into their nations."   *Genesis 10:5*

From these nations emerged unique cultures and accompanying cultural norms and characteristics. God spoke of the Chaldeans as "that fierce and impetuous people" (Habakkuk 1:6b). The Edomites were known for their 'arrogance' (Obadiah 1:3); the Amalekites for their 'cruelty' (Deuteronomy 25:18). There was a time He said of His own people, Israel:

> *"this people draw near with their words and honor Me with their lip service, but they remove their hearts far from Me, and their reverence for Me consists of tradition learned by rote"*
> Isaiah 29:13

Yet among them, God highlights some of the descendants of Issachar, "men who understood the times, with knowledge of what Israel should do" (1 Chronicles 12:32). These men retained godly lifestyles, while others around them were becoming captivated by the surrounding hedonistic culture.

To me, culture is the emerging accumulation of 'rules' and behavioural 'norms' established to foster a particular kind of society, sharing distinct goals and values. Unfortunately, each human culture from every generation is somewhat tainted, and thus darkened by sinful tendencies.

> *"For all that is in the world, the lust of the flesh and the lust of the eyes and the boastful pride of life, is not from the Father, but is from the world."*   1 John 2:16

Thankfully, it goes on to add, "the world is passing away, and *also* its lusts; but the one who does the will of God abides forever" (1 John 2:17). In order to live forever, people are called to become 'disciples' of Jesus, a 'people for God's own possession' (Titus 2:14b). Titus 2: 11-12 explains,

For the grace of God has appeared, bringing salvation to all men, instructing us to deny ungodliness and worldly desires and to live sensibly, righteously and godly in the present age.

This means we are to live differently than our surrounding culture's values dictate, and pursue a higher biblical standard of conduct. James 1:27 offers,

"Pure and undefiled religion in the sight of our God and Father is this: to visit orphans and widows in their distress, and to keep oneself unstained by the world. "

The overarching premise of this book is to promote the supreme value of responding to Jesus; to let Him create a 'biblical culture' within you, in order to serve His Kingdom purposes toward the needy, while remaining 'unstained' by whatever culture He places you in! Sadly, this way of living is described in Matthew 7:14 as 'narrow, and there are few who find it'. Those who do, will discover a deeper and richer experience of living, filled with 'joy unspeakable'!

Culture makes me think of *freewill*. By choice, God does not 'control' everything, but He is 'in charge' of everything. He permits us to choose freely, either for or against His will in all circumstances. Because He knows the beginning from the end, He already sees our choices, and so He rightly uses us all within the orchestration of His larger purposes through human history.

So why does *culture* bring this to mind? Well, without freewill, we would simply be 'robots', doing God's bidding, without choice. And that is precisely what I think of when I look at human cultures. Some say 'religion' is restrictive, but to me, there is so much more freedom in living a biblical culture, and enjoying being a part of His activities, than the more robotic lifestyles of earthly cultures.

If you are willing to think of this objectively, you will agree how indoctrinated and 'locked in' we are to the dictates and whims of our culture. We mechanically become just like those around us. We wear the acceptable clothes, say the acceptable words, move about by the acceptable means, and basically conform to whatever is going on around us. And even if we say we are *counter-cultural*, we follow the distinct patterns and ways of the counter-cultural 'rules'.

It is sad, really, how much we miss in richness of living. How much more wonderful to conform to the wondrous ways of the only One who chooses perfectly for our best, who loves us unconditionally and seeks the greatest good for all.

Perhaps two of the greatest factors causing most to refuse really living for Him in holistic biblical ways are the magnetic draw of worldly culture, and man's propensity toward sin. To live a biblical culture requires many choices every day to 'deny our self and take up our cross' (Mark 8:34), surrendering to His ways instead. Jesus demonstrated it in everyday living as He ministered to the people around Him. For example:

> *And it came about as He said these things, one of the women in the crowd raised her voice, and said to Him, "Blessed is the womb that bore You, and the breasts at which You nursed." But He [Jesus] said, "On the contrary, blessed are those who hear the word of God, and observe it."   Luke 11:27b-28*

At every point He was alert to what was 'actually' true in a situation, and not swayed by the thoughts of the crowd.

Central to living a biblical lifestyle is the concept, 'not of the world, but sent into the world' (John 17:11-21). It demands transformed living. "Therefore if any man is in Christ, he is a new creature; the old things passed away; behold, new things have come" (2 Corinthians

5:17). Jesus said, "I have come as light into the world, that everyone who believes in Me may not remain in darkness" (John 12:46). The 'darkness' comes from all the little things tugging us away from God's will on any given day; our cell phones and other gadgets, our opinions about those around us, our apathy toward difficult things, our secret sins. But mostly, darkness occurs from our lack of sufficient love for Jesus, which would override the ever so subtle, yet insidious temptations our culture pushes upon us.

Peter said it well:

"Beloved, I urge you as aliens and strangers to abstain from fleshly lusts which wage war against the soul. Keep your behaviour excellent among the Gentiles, so that in the thing in which they slander you as evildoers, they may because of your good deeds, as they observe them, glorify God in the day of visitation."   1 Peter 2:11-12

The sheer beauty of living a biblical culture is how effective it is for His Kingdom. Look at some of the responses to Jesus' lifestyle. "And Jesus kept increasing in wisdom and stature, and in favor with God and men" (Luke 2:52). His lifestyle and manner of speaking was such that he gained the respect of the people around Him, while living fully for God. "And they were amazed at His teaching; for He was teaching them as one having authority, and not as the scribes" (Mark 1:22). The things He spoke of were penetratingly true and convicting, yet simultaneously compelling and inspiring to real seekers. Following Jesus' example of living biblically instead of culturally, we too can be used effectively by God.

'Loving your neighbour as yourself' (Luke 10:27b) is a primary culturally biblical mandate which 'works' powerfully and effectively all over the world, while human cultures continually wrestle with issues of race, class and tribe, seemingly unable to come to proper resolve. Such is the impact of a life given over to a biblical culture!

Yes, you will face persecution, as Jesus Himself experienced, even to His death. This is part of the plan of God, which He has you participate in, placing choices before every soul to choose either for or against Him. As disciples, we share in both the sufferings and eternal blessings of God. Paul's own biblical life pursuits highlighted the blessings and the sufferings of life with Jesus when he wrote,

> *"that I may know Him, and the power of His resurrection and the fellowship of His sufferings, being conformed to His death;" Philippians 3:10*

Living the life of a disciple is bound to elicit some degree of persecution, for it is not in the sinful nature of man to desire the things of God. John explained,

> *For everyone who does evil hates the light, and does not come to the light, lest his deeds should be exposed.* John 3:20

But it is in the very process of 'denying ourselves, and our sin' that the power of God's authority manifests, drawing others to Him through our sacrificial obedience.

God has been faithful to me, a sinner, and in the midst of it all, relentlessly restores me back onto the narrow path I daily stray from. I know He will do the same for you, if you are willing to pay attention to the details of your life, and carefully choose Him in what you think, say and do as you go about your day with Him, regardless of what your culture tempts you to do.

PERSONAL [BEING]

Jesus well expressed the foremost commandment,

AND YOU SHALL LOVE THE LORD YOUR GOD WITH ALL YOUR HEART, AND WITH ALL YOUR SOUL, AND WITH ALL YOUR MIND, AND WITH ALL YOUR STRENGTH.   *Mark 12:30*

In this section I will try to share my thoughts and heart on the paramount value of intimately and completely BEING in love with God, and becoming 'his own possession'. Loving Him deeply is the best incentive for driving us from our sinful tendencies, and toward a surrendered life of allegiance to Him alone.

SALVATION

When Eve first disobeyed God
in the Garden of Eden,
we all lost two things
that every human
through all of human history
spends their life trying to recover.
The first is UNCONDITIONAL LOVE,
and the second is SELF-WORTH.

So with these thoughts in mind, let's step back to the beginning of this journey of falling in love with Jesus enough to live beyond that of a 'believer', as a true disciple, living out a biblical culture in darkening days. Here are some of the things I have found important about the process of salvation itself.

Love

It all begins with LOVE! It is not a human love. It does not originate with us. "We love, because He first loved us" (1 John 4:19). Sometimes love is difficult to comprehend, especially for those who have never had the privilege of growing up with loving parents, or having those around them who expressed how valuable they were. But in His great mercy, God places things before each of us through nature and other people, to expose His Presence and love to us in ways that draw us toward Him.

Jesus specifically explained to the Jews, "No one can come to Me, unless the Father who sent Me draws him" (John 6:44a). To the Romans the Apostle Paul declared, "But God demonstrates His own love toward us, in that while we were yet sinners, Christ died for us" (Romans 5:8). He could have used any means to procure our salvation, but He chose a most deep and sacrificial way, so we could comprehend and become convinced of the purity and genuineness of His perfect love. What glorious truths concerning the depth of God's love demonstrated to bring us back to the state we were originally intended to enjoy, before sinful disobedience separated us from Him.

Given this, part of the necessary and beautiful process of salvation is our own journey of falling in love with Him. Now I don't mean that 'wow, she's smokin' hot; I'd love to have her for myself', or 'he's so attractive, I wonder if he will even notice me' kind of love. That is more a self-centered hope for personal gratification. I am speaking here of a much deeper and truer kind of falling in love.

Falling in love with the very Creator God means taking the time and interest to become acquainted with His pure Character. It involves developing a sense of awe, a deep respect and a growing honour for who He is and has always been. By reading His Word and interacting with Him in prayer, you begin to observe that He is the embodiment of love and light and wisdom and truth. He is infinite, yet intimate, palatial, yet personal, lofty, yet lowly, peaceful, yet provocative, heavenly, yet humble, incomprehensible, yet knowable.

It means becoming convinced of His Being, His utmost intimate love for us, and falling in love with every aspect of His Holy nature. For without falling head over heels in love with the Triune God, we are most certain to fall short of becoming a disciple of His, and miss many of the deeper blessings which come from living out a biblical culture. Falling in love with God extends through the entire process of receiving eternal salvation from Him, by the finished work of Christ in the power of His Holy Spirit.

I would now like to explain my simple understanding of receiving this glorious gift of God, called salvation. This is where life becomes worth living; the grass gets greener and the sun shines brighter for the rest of your brief but newly blessed journey through life on planet earth. This is where you come to experience the fullness of His penetrating love and begin to comprehend the real meaning and purpose of life itself!

Separation

Let me first say a bit about the meaning of life as I have come to see it. When Eve first disobeyed God in the Garden of Eden, we all lost two things that every human through all of human history spends their life trying to recover. The first is UNCONDITIONAL LOVE, and the second is SELF WORTH. Eve, then Adam in disobeying God, for the first time wondered if He was angry with them and hid themselves in naked shame from His sight. For the first time they felt the weight of sin from a place of disobedience, and sensed a new distance from His complete Holiness.

From that moment on, mankind has been 'separated' from Holy God by sin and in need of supernatural restoration by the removal of that sin. The cry of every human heart since that moment remains: 'Does anyone love me?' and 'Do I have any value?' A gang member stays loyal to his crew by an underlying sense that the fellow members have some sort of care and use for him. An artist paints, hoping someone will see the worth and person inside of her. An executive directs a company to achieve recognition and success in order to have worth, and possessions that will attract friends, a pseudo form of love... it goes on through all aspects of every culture on earth. Almost everything we do, both good and evil, are in some fashion related to an unending pursuit of these two illusive desires.

And this is the heart of the gospel (good news) of Jesus Christ! God sent Jesus into our world to demonstrate His unconditional love toward each one of us, and to restore our true value and purpose in the community of fellowship with Himself and those around us.

Salvation is the receiving of that unconditional love from God in the depth of your soul as it was originally intended to be. It is the recovery of that eternal relationship Adam and Eve had before their wilful disobedience caused mankind to be separated from Him. It brings to life the significant worth of your being set on earth with the gifts you have been given. It sets you on a new mission of meaning and purpose found in conjoining with the activity of God to your generation. But more of that later...

There are actually a few things I see which must occur prior to salvation. First you must come to believe there is a God/Creator of the universe in the first place, and begin to seek Him out.

Hebrews 11:6b states, "for he who comes to God must believe that He is, and that He is a rewarder of those who seek Him." Without acknowledging His existence, you have no one worth believing in, or receiving salvation from.

He will help you to find Him if you are genuine and willing in your search.

Second, you must come to admit and accept that you are, in fact, a sinner. That is, you do things wrong, things in disobedience to God's perfect will, things that prevent you from ever being able to come into the presence of a pure and holy God. You must accept that you are therefore destined to be forever separated from God and there is absolutely NOTHING you can do to change that, apart from His saving grace!

Restoration

Once you agree with God that you are a sinner, lost, and destined to be separated from Him forever, the GOOD NEWS about Jesus Christ kicks in! John 3:16 recounts, "For God so loved the world [you and me], that He gave His only begotten Son". Why? Well, through His great love and desire for all of His created beings to be restored to a sinless state and live forever in His Presence, He provided His Son as the Saviour, able to make sufficient payment for our sins! This one precious act gives us the only opportunity to come into the very Presence of God again, as though we were sinless and blameless in His sight.

Restoration from an eternally separate state is offered freely in every generation to every person on the earth. That includes you and me! This is why it is called the "Good News". God's offer of salvation derives its ability from the sacrifice of Jesus, leaving heaven to dwell among us for a season, leading a sinless life acceptable to God, taking our sins upon Himself, dying on a cross at the hands of sinful man, but rising from the dead three days later. Having conquered the power of sin and death, He gives us the ability to receive that same power over sin and death, and to ultimately live forever sinless in the Presence of the Living God, free from the chains of this world.

Now if you have truly acknowledged you are a sinner in need of a Saviour, you should have an accompanying regret about your sinfulness. Without true remorse, you will not long for a Saviour, but perhaps just the potential hope for a 'free ticket' to heaven.

So the next step in seeking the Saviour is a willingness to turn away from your abhorrent sin through a process called 'repentance'. Repentance is basically having sufficient sorrow over your sin that you determine to reject those sinful ways for the much better ways of God, as laid out in the Bible.

The simple admonition of Scripture is: "repent and believe" (Mark 1:15; Acts 20:21). Upon true repentance and placing genuine faith in God, through the sacrifice of Jesus Christ on your behalf, you receive His marvellous gift of salvation! Your slate is wiped clean, and the Holy Spirit of God is placed within you to help you now "consider yourselves to be dead to sin, but alive to God in Christ Jesus" (Romans 6:11) through the balance of your earthly life.

From this moment on, your life shifts from receiving Jesus as your Saviour, to making Him the Lord of your life. You are now called to become a servant, and He becomes your King. "Therefore if any man is in Christ he is a new creature; the old things passed away; behold new things have come" (2 Corinthians 5:17).

LORDSHIP

It is selfless and
Kingdom-centered.
It is indeed a 'narrow way',
but it leads to SUCH A LIFE!

Once admission of guilt has been confessed and Christ Jesus accepted as Saviour, the rest of your life becomes a series of choices. The extent to which you surrender your will to His and entrust Him to lead you each day, will determine whether you attain to the average life of a *believer* or the blessed life of a *disciple*.

'Dying to sin', 'denying self' and being 'alive to Christ' (Matthew 16:24; Romans 6:11), as I have said, are essential components to living a biblical culture. Some merely try changing some of their behaviour, to become 'better' people and 'do the right things', to 'go to church' and 'eliminate some bad habits', but fall short on the 'alive to Christ' part. We speak boldly of Christ as Saviour, but tend to only pay lip service to much of His Lordship. By not surrendering into His authority and charge of your daily lifestyle, you will fall short of becoming His disciple.

This reminds me of a funny skit we used to perform while leading a Christian singing and drama team in Kenya, East Africa. A pastor would be standing alone on stage. Someone would enter making airplane sounds; arms spread wide, acting like a plane. The pastor would ask what they were doing, to which they would reply, "Why, I am an airplane!" The pastor would gently respond that just because they looked and sounded like an airplane, that didn't make them an actual airplane." This would be repeated by another sounding and acting like a chicken, followed by someone sounding and acting like a Christian. The moral of the story, of course, was to teach that 'acting' like a Christian does not make you one. Without the deep, genuine abhorrence of your sin, you are likely to simply mask it with the appearance of Christian actions, behaviours and activities, but lack in the true power of God from a surrendered heart and life.

So how does Christ become Lord? Well, it involves a new commitment, beautifully pictured and likened to the vows of marriage between a couple, for a lifelong and single-focused relationship of intimate love, trust and loyalty. We are commanded by Jesus to

"LOVE THE LORD GOD WITH ALL YOUR HEART, AND WITH ALL YOUR SOUL, AND WITH ALL YOUR MIND, AND WITH ALL YOUR STRENGTH."   *Mark 12:30*

Part of that equation is the acceptance of the supreme authority of God for both your personal well-being and also your service for His Kingdom activity on earth. This leads to a life of servanthood, through an accompanying command to

"LOVE YOUR NEIGHBOR AS YOURSELF."   *Mark 12:31*

On these two commands lie the very foundation blocks of Christian living as a disciple of Jesus; experiencing a sufficient depth of intimate love for God that you will forever possess a willingness to both 'deny yourself' and 'take up your cross to follow Him' (Matthew 16:24) for the eternal good of others.

In Luke 18:35-43 we see a blind man crying out, "Jesus, Son of David, have mercy on me!" (verse 38), to which Jesus replies, "Receive your sight; your faith has made you well" (verse 42). Immediately the man with new sight 'followed' Jesus. Believing is simply not enough; a Christ-ian is a 'follower' of the teachings of Christ.

Lordship is an extremely difficult reality. It takes precedence over all cultural norms. It requires unwavering loyalty and daily sacrifice. It is selfless and Kingdom-centered. It is indeed a 'narrow way', but it leads to SUCH A LIFE!

Luke's gospel recites three clear prerequisites for being a disciple of Christ, in effect allowing Him to be Lord of your life. The first is to love God more than any other human relationship.

"If anyone comes to Me, and does not hate his own father and mother and wife and children and brothers and sisters, yes, and even his own life, he cannot be My disciple." Luke 14:26

Second,

"Whoever does not carry his own cross and come after Me cannot be My disciple." Verse 27

As Christ surrendered into the will of His Father, and suffered the pain and persecution of the cross, so we must give Him this kind of supreme allegiance. Third,

"no one of you can be My disciple who does not give up all his own possessions." Verse 33

We are called to give up everything we might hold on to that would hold us back from whatever He directs us to do.

These are not idealistic goals or suggestions, they are practical necessities. It all boils down to rearranging our priorities and developing our wholeheartedness toward God. For if we are not willing to go where He leads, say what He prompts and do what He sets our hands to, then we are 'actually' living for ourselves. In essence we are trying to make Him OUR servant, to bless OUR desires and action.

These are sobering thoughts my dear friends, but we are told to 'count the cost' (Luke 14:28) before we build, lest we fall short and become a ridiculed people. I can tell you with all sincerity that the cost/benefit analysis of my own life weighs heavily in favour of the benefits! My life is filled with His activity, the 'fruit from much labour', and I enjoy great joy and peace in my life from loving my God more than anything or anyone else. It truly is a blessed life!

HOLINESS

Without sufficient reverence for God,
there is almost too strong a pull
from the prevailing
worldly culture,
causing us to justify
its various forms
in our life.

One of the characteristics of Almighty God is His holiness. Gaining a comprehension of His Holy Nature should become a compelling factor for repentance and humble surrender into His Lordship over your life. It is not just a trait or quality, but an essence of His Being. God is distinctly above all else and uniquely set apart in holiness. He is morally and eternally pure, and cannot accept sin in His Presence. Habakkuk rightly noted, "Thine eyes are too pure to approve evil, and Thou canst not look on wickedness with favor" (1:13a). His Holy Nature should humble us and produce a genuine sense of shame for our sin, resulting in a complete willingness to turn from that sin, rather than enjoying its small fleeting pleasures.

One helpful picture, in this regard, is found in Isaiah 6:1-5:

"In the year of King Uzziah's death, I saw the Lord sitting on a throne, lofty and exalted, with the train of His robe filling the temple. Seraphim stood above Him, each having six wings; with two he covered his face, and with two he covered his feet, and with two he flew.

And one called out to another and said, "Holy, Holy, Holy, is the Lord of hosts, the whole earth is full of His glory." And the foundations of the thresholds trembled at the voice of him who called out, while the temple was filling with smoke. Then I said, "Woe is me, for I am ruined! Because I am a man of unclean lips, and I live among a people of unclean lips; for my eyes have seen the King, the Lord of hosts."

The year of Uzziah's death marked a pivotal point in history, where things turned from better to worse for God's disobedient people. In this vision given to Isaiah, he is penetrated so intensely by the holiness of Almighty God that his sin completely and utterly overwhelms him. Isaiah would serve His people as a prophet in a season when his message would be rejected. The culture around him would disintegrate while he was simultaneously called to remain faithful to God's ways. It was the Holiness of God and his reverence for the Almighty which became the motivating factor in Isaiah remaining true to his personal calling and public message.

The other striking feature of this passage to me is the posture of the angelic Seraphim! Two of his six wings are relegated to averting his eyes from the holy Presence of God. Two others serve to cover the feet, a symbol of the earthly part of life. Imagine if we had such a holy posture, how we would disdainfully turn from so much of what we culturally engage in during the course of a day.

I will be forever grateful to the saints at Hopedale Bible Chapel in Oakville, Ontario for helping to implant in my young life a deep sense of the holiness of God. After God miraculously rescued me from the path I was taking toward the drug culture around me, I repented and gave my life to Christ at Calvary Baptist Church. While they provided me with an initial love for the Word of God and an acceptance of me as a young long-haired teenager, it was when I began attending the Bible

Chapel that I really caught a clearer picture of life lived in awe of God, and the depth of reverence for Him.

They demonstrated to me this passionate reverence for God; one of the pillars of my faith which has carried me through to this day. Without sufficient reverence for God, there is almost too strong a pull from the prevailing worldly culture, causing us to justify its various forms in our life. It was in those quiet early gatherings for Communion, to remember His Son, that it became more important to me for God's Spirit not be grieved, than to justify my sin before His throne of glory. I remember weeping over my sins, so burdened was I that I was disappointing Him. Without this prevailing sense of hatred for sin, the ways of the world can daily envelope you and seduce you back into its values and norms.

INTIMACY

I have found that you will
get out of the Bible
whatever you go into it for.
You will not become
intimate with the Father
simply by getting
a 'thought for the day',
or a 'rule to obey'.

When I began to put these thoughts together, I saw 'intimacy' as the first chapter, but then God reminded me that intimacy with Himself is central to every aspect of developing and living out a more biblical lifestyle. It plays a vital role in every topic covered by this book.

Later in life, John insightfully shared,

> *"And we have come to know and have believed the love which God has for us. God is love, and the one who abides in love abides in God, and God abides in Him."*　　1 John 4:16

As my wife often says, 'Love is a verb'. It should not only deeply permeate our soul, but emanate from us in all our actions. It is born out of a growing intimacy of faithful unadulterated love with the Father, and produces in us the kind of loyalty necessary to guard against our natural sinful tendencies.

Intimacy with the Godhead develops from being knit together through a close association over a long period of time, sometimes referred to in the Bible as 'fellowship' (see 1 John 1:3). In Old Testament times only the High Priest was permitted once a year into the Holy of Holies (see Hebrews 9:7), within the Tabernacle of His Presence among His people, Israel. But when Jesus died on the cross, "the veil of the temple was torn in two from top [heaven] to bottom [earth]" (Mark 15:38), symbolizing the sufficiency of Christ's sacrifice to provide us access into the very Presence of Holy God.

We now have unfettered access through the completed work of Christ to our 'Abba Father' (Romans 8:15b). We no longer need a human priest to mediate on our behalf, for Jesus, seated at the right hand of God, is now our Mediator. Hebrews 10:22 recommends, "let us draw near with a sincere heart in full assurance of faith".

Jesus spent about half His time of ministry with 'the multitudes', the general crowd variously motivated to come, see and hear Him, and perhaps witness a miracle or two. The other half He spent intimately with 12 disciples, and among them, extra private time with the three who would be given the awesome task of writing some of the New Testament Scriptures. After delivering concepts to the crowds in parabolic language, He would inevitably 'turn to His disciples' (e.g. Luke 10:23) and explain the deep meaning of the message to them privately.

Today we are afforded the same kind of intimacy with Jesus through reading and responding to His Word. As we interact with Him in prayer, while we study, we draw closer in our understanding and appreciation of Him. I have found that you will get out of the Bible whatever you go into it for. You will not become intimate with the Father simply by getting a 'thought for the day', or a 'rule to obey'. Intimacy is accomplished through a melding of souls in private seasons alone with the Father, withholding nothing from Him, and denying nothing from Him. I pray you get a close enough glimpse of His Majesty to come completely and utterly 'undone' as Isaiah did.

OBEDIENCE

He was always the influencer,
never the influenced.

The trouble with 'tolerance' is
it deceptively implies 'condoning',
and inevitably demands 'acceptance'.

Obedience flows from Lordship, born of a growing intimacy of love with our Holy God. 1 Peter 1:13 reads,

"Therefore, gird your minds for action, keep sober in spirit, fix your hope completely on the grace to be brought to you at the revelation of Jesus Christ. As obedient children, do not be conformed to the former lusts which were yours in your ignorance, but like the Holy One who called you, be holy yourselves also in all your behaviour; because it is written, "YOU SHALL BE HOLY, FOR I AM HOLY."

Chapter 2:11-12 continues,

"Beloved, I urge you as aliens and strangers to abstain from fleshly lusts, which wage war against the soul. Keep your behaviour excellent among the Gentiles, so that in the thing in which they slander you as evildoers, they may on account of your good deeds, as they observe them, glorify God in the day of visitation."

Matthew 10:16 adds,

"Behold, I send you out as sheep in the midst of wolves; therefore be shrewd as serpents, and innocent as doves."

So what does all of this look like in everyday life? Well, Jesus went to a lot of parties and hung out with those whom many church leaders shunned or condemned as 'sinners'. But He always seemed to dominate the atmosphere, offering penetrating questions and giving truthful advice. He did not conform to their ways, but 'made the most of every opportunity' (Colossians 4:5b). He remained obedient to the Father, while fully engaged with the sinner. He was always the influencer, never the influenced!

In verses 2-6 of Colossians 4, Paul lays out a number of practices to follow as your day unfolds: 'Be devoted to prayer, keep alert for God's activity, maintain a thankful attitude, look for openings to share clearly about Christ and His Word, and let those words be gracious, responding properly to people.'

Regretfully, it appears the church in general is experiencing another generational cycle of decline from holy living and separation from the ways of the surrounding culture. Yet I have observed that every third or fourth generation God amazingly provides a rather sweeping movement of the Holy Spirit, often amongst the youth, to rescue His people from the cycle of decline, so I am hopeful. Perhaps in our day, another spiritually fervent generation will emerge, but this may, in fact, be the last downward spiral, as the signs more than ever in history point to the end of a dying world.

As prevailing cultures penetrate the Christian culture, some so-called followers of Christ can worship God on Sunday, live entirely for self on Monday, get plastered in the bar on Friday, and then take home and sleep with a sister in Christ. While these things have occurred through the ages, they have become more 'normal' as the light dims and the darkness is permitted to encroach into the minds and hearts of successive generations of 'believers'.

A new 'Christian' mantra, I have heard over and over lately among North American 'believing' youth, can be summarized as: "What does it matter?" "Why bother living different from our culture? Why not enjoy the night life and a little sexual freedom? What harm is there in a few crude jokes and some foul language? It is just being normal… and anyway, the risk of being alienated is too great; and you're not allowed to speak about religion anyway!"

This generation has been harassed into conforming to the world's image; to remain silent about Christ and His love; to be 'tolerant' of all things. The trouble with *tolerance* is it deceptively implies *condoning*, and eventually demands *acceptance*.

Through counselling some of these young 'evangelicals', lured into silence and partial cultural conformity, I have sadly observed that they end up experiencing much of the same angst, disillusionment, frustration, lack of purpose and lostness as their unbelieving peers in the worldly culture around them.

Now contrast this with a life altering experience I had while attending an international Prayer Summit in Hong Kong. A number of Christian leaders gathered to better discern God's movement around the globe. While there, I met a truly inspiring young man (many actually, but this one in particular transformed my journey). Growing up, he had faithfully followed his culture, excelled in school, obtained a superior job in a profitable career-oriented company and acquired a very nice home. But when he met Christ through the ministry of the Kowloon Cell Church, the impact of his newly found intimacy with Jesus shifted his whole being. As he learned about the life of a disciple he became more compelled by Jesus than his own culture.

At one point he asked me an unusual question about the people of my church in Canada. He asked, "What do your church people do at night? How many nights do they serve the church?" To my somewhat rationalized, then apologetic response he commented, "Why would you want to do anything other than serve the church when you are not obligated to be at your workplace?" I later discovered that he not only served the church seven nights a week, but had kept cutting back on his work schedule to the point where he was working only two days a week for his employer. He gave up his home and possessions, choosing to live instead on a cot in a rooming house, with all of his belongings in a backpack under the bed... all so he could expend more of his time, energy and giftings helping to evangelize his neighbourhood and increase the Kingdom of God! It so impacted me that I determined to return to Canada more attentive and responsive to God's Word and ways. His demonstration of obedience, by living a biblical culture over his own strongly pervasive secular culture, transformed my thinking and propelled me beyond my own deceptively 'lulling' society.

True obedience cooperates with God's activity, as He masterfully uses your biblical culture to engage the world around you in compelling ways. So for me it is important to stay alert to His activity, jump into it as He permits and guides me, and then share the wonderful results with others! This is the path to becoming a true 'light in the world' (Matthew 5:14).

LIGHT

Essentially, we are meant to offer
a clear difference
from the prevailing culture
that is significantly 'brighter'
and thus appealing,

One of the amazing images God uses to demonstrate our intended effect on the surrounding culture is that of 'light'. Light always eliminates darkness. Darkness has absolutely no power to obscure light. Wherever light shines, darkness dissipates. Light is the polar opposite of darkness and is used by Jesus to illustrate both the transformative difference our life is meant to exude, and the infinite power of true light over the ways of darkness.

Ephesians 5 clearly informs us that imitating our culture excludes us from joining in the 'light' of God's kingdom. Speaking about the actions of the disobedient, and the accompanying dire consequences, verses 7-8 relate, "Therefore do not be partakers with them; for you were formerly darkness, but now you are light in the Lord; walk as children of light". Jesus established the church of 'true believers' (saints) to shine as lights in the darkness. Essentially, we are meant to offer a clear difference from the prevailing culture that is significantly 'brighter' and thus appealing, as the worldly culture falls short of providing sufficient meaning and purpose.

When the church prides itself on being believers who effectively live *like* the surrounding culture, what is really taking place is the light being hidden. Matthew 5: 14-15 clearly explains,

"You are the light of the world. A city set on a hill cannot be hidden. Nor do men light a lamp, and put it under the peck-measure [basket], but on the lampstand; and it gives light to all who are in the house."

Individual Christians (*followers* of the teachings of Christ) are awarded salvation not through preference, for God shows no partiality (Romans 2:11), but for the mission of shining as 'lights' to the nations. Matthew 5:16 goes on to encourage,

"Let your light shine before men in such a way that they may see your good works, and glorify your Father who is in heaven."

The world should not look upon us and declare 'hypocrite', or 'I know non-Christians who live better than him'. Rather, 'there is something about him that is different, and I long for what he has!'

I was recently at a morning men's study where a godly man was relating his salvation story. Growing up with no church background, what was key for him was a fellow employee who obviously had a much better and more fulfilling life than himself. The *light* of this man was delightfully modeled in such an effectively compelling manner, that he was drawn to God for his own life. Now he has become a *beacon* for others!

Jesus was amazing His culture even at 12 years old with his wisdom of questions and answers. They were awed by the power He exhibited and the authority with which He conducted Himself (see Luke 2:41-47). They were impressed at His teaching and many repented as a result, beginning their own journey of becoming light in a dark world.

Young Christians, beware of trying to be 'modernistic'; of attempting to be *mainstream* in your lifestyle. Our mission is not to blend in with our culture, nor is it to be different from it, but to live in a biblical manner wherever you reside. The *difference* will become apparent all on its own. The result, the litmus test, of shining with biblical living, Jesus said, is a dual effect. One will be the repentance of some; the other, He informs us, is being hated by others (John 15:18) and mistreated (Luke 6:28). He unfolds this further,

> *"And this is the judgment, that the light is come into the world, and men loved the darkness rather than the light; for their deeds were evil. For everyone who does evil hates the light, and does not come to the light, lest his deeds should be exposed."*
> *John 3:19-20*

Jesus exhorts us to persevere with the negative, and consoles our spirit with the positive;

> *"If the world hates you, you know that it has hated Me before it hated you. If you were of the world, the world would love its own; but because you are not of the world, but I chose you out of the world, therefore the world hates you. Remember the word that I said to you, 'A slave is not greater than his master.' If they persecuted Me, they will also persecute you; if they kept My word, they will keep yours also."*   *John 15:18-20*

I remember with fondness the countless hours spent on my bed, reading Bible verses for the very first time. For me they were astounding to my mind, revolutionizing to my spirit at the tender age of 16, and transforming to my soul. Each truth penetrated me so deeply and profoundly, as I gained new knowledge of 'real' truth and how to let it change my life from darkness to light, from earthly to heavenly, from meagre to amazing! I trust you will discover the same in your own walk of living in love with Jesus.

GROWTH

We choose His ways,
and He enables us to
accomplish them!

Now becoming a 'light of the world', effective disciple does not happen overnight. While the commitment to being a disciple can be a single decision, there is a lengthy progression to becoming one as well. In essence, we grow into one as we obey Him over time. His own disciples left everything to follow Him, and yet they argued along the path as to who was greatest among them... making progress... needing growth.

In 2 Peter 1 there is an extraordinary progression for spiritual growth given by the Lord, which proved very helpful to me in my own journey. Commencing with verse 5 it outlines,

> *"applying all diligence, in your faith supply moral excellence, and in your moral excellence, knowledge; and in your knowledge, self-control, and in your self-control, perseverance, and in your perseverance, godliness; and in your godliness, brotherly kindness, and in your brotherly kindness, love." Verses 5-7*

Why is *moral excellence* the first thing to work on? Why not knowledge, or love? When you fall in love with Jesus, that is, when you surrender to the call of God through His Spirit, you spiritually die to your 'self'. Coming to faith in Christ is not a mere decision to believe He exists. It is meant to be a life transforming experience forever. At the point of conversion you lose three friends, who become your enemies: the world, the flesh and the devil. Where you once catered to these, you now turn from them in repentance from your former sinful life. The world goes on feeding you lies about what is of value in this life. Your own flesh continues to produce evil thoughts, desires and actions. And the devil has a new passion to destroy your *moral excellence* by devious tactics at opportune moments, wherever you are most vulnerable.

Thankfully, we also take on three new allies, the Father, Son and Holy Spirit. They are overwhelmingly more powerful than the three foes, so victory is now obtainable. In this new battle for moral excellence there is now 'no temptation beyond what you are able to bear', for

"God is faithful, who will not allow you to be tempted beyond what you are able, but with the temptation will provide the way of escape also, that you may be able to endure it."
1 Corinthians 10:13

If you have truly taken Him to be the Lord and center of your life, then "the old things passed away; behold, new things have come" (2 Corinthians 5:17b). This is why confessing sin and turning from it is integral to the conversion experience. Every immoral, self-focused thought, desire and action is to be laid down, and a whole new life of surrender to the ways of Jesus is taken up. Even without *knowledge* to guide you, your conscience pricks your mind and heart to cease and desist from all immorality, and begin a *born again* life characterized by *moral excellence*.

Many who simply say a *salvation* prayer in order to 'make it into heaven' may in fact never get there. Some may, *as through fire*, but miss out on all the glorious living there is to be had in a deep loving relationship with God, through the Saviour, by the enlivening power of the Spirit!

Now moral excellence is followed by *knowledge*, the growing body of information you are now receiving with new *spiritual eyes*. It is imperative to begin the lifetime process of growing in knowledge and understanding of the morally excellent surrendered life! It feels like infancy at first, but develops into a whole new biblical view about the world around you; why it exists, what purpose you have in it, the meaning of living, and life beyond this *foretaste of glory divine*.

New believers are often encouraged too early to 'get out there' and 'serve with love'. This is like asking a newborn baby to construct a building or become an elder! More appropriately, here is where you commence Mary's Bible School experience as she "was listening to the Lord's word, seated at His feet" (Luke 10:39). Here it is that you grapple with internalizing things like:

> *"laying aside falsehood, SPEAK TRUTH, EACH ONE of you, WITH HIS NEIGHBOR, for we are members of one another. Be angry, and yet DO NOT SIN; do not let the sun go down on your anger, and do not give the devil an opportunity. Let him who steals steal no longer; but rather let him labor, performing with his own hands what is good, in order that he may have something to share with him who has need. Let no unwholesome word proceed from your mouth, but only such a word as is good for edification according to the need of the moment, that it might give grace to those who hear."*   *Ephesians 4:25-29*

My goodness, there is so much *knowledge* to digest in that one passage, it could take years to even grasp the significance of each thought! These verses include a life purpose defined for 'work'; there is a case for honesty, for wholesome speech; there is a valuation for forgiveness… and the list goes on. Knowledge is paramount to understanding the very heart of God toward us, for us and through us.

Once knowledge begins to penetrate we become fraught with new moral dilemmas. Knowing right and living right are two very different matters, thus *self-control* follows logically in the Lord's progression. Turning from sin, and responding to the new information we receive from His Word, requires His strengthening power for self-control. It is by His power, and yet He gives us free will in our choices, which is why it is referred to as 'self'-control. We choose His ways and He enables us to accomplish them!

As we grow in knowledge, we are more deeply confronted with our own sin; far beyond the conscience that pricks every man facing the moral issues of life. Now that we have spiritual goodness dwelling within us, we are freshly drawn to please our Father in heaven, more than any earthly creature. Every sin comes to light, and we must grow in our ability to resist the world, our own flesh and the devil, with the overcoming power of the Father, the Son and the Holy Spirit.

The Apostle Paul outlined his own strategy:

"I buffet my body and make it my slave, lest possibly, after I have preached to others, I myself should be disqualified"
1 Corinthians 9:27

This step of growing in self-control extends beyond our own sin, to focused attention on how we deal with those around us. Thus we grow in determination not to judge outsiders, as they are judged already (see 1 Corinthians 5:12-13), but to influence them toward Christ. To them, we exhibit self-control by being 'salt and light', pointing the way to the Godhead, rather than merely criticizing their faults. We learn to hold our tongue, and wrestle its evil intent to the ground. Toward fellow followers *"caught in any trespass, you who are spiritual, restore such a one in a spirit of gentleness; each one looking to yourself, lest you too be tempted."* Galatians 6:1b

What else could you expect, then, to follow in this journey but *perseverance*! He cautions us: "do not grow weary of doing good" (2 Thessalonians 3:13). Our natural tendency, given difficult circumstances, is to back away; to quit, proclaiming the weariness of it all, and throwing in the towel. Fortunately, "greater is He who is in you than he who is in the world" (1 John 4:4).

Romans 5:4 reminds us also, that 'perseverance produces proven character'. Following these progressive steps over time turns our growing efforts into a culturally biblical lifestyle, so needed in this darkening world.

As the battle rages for faith to produce moral excellence and self-control, the spiritual experiences of His strengthening power will lend themselves to an increase in *godliness*. Despite the struggles, we begin to see with spiritual eyes the supreme value of walking with and for Him, rather than in isolation of worldly pursuits. And so, *godliness* begins to make its mark on our soul, now shaping our character, and the self-control and perseverance start paying off.

Finally, as His nature tips the balance over our own futile nature, *brotherly kindness* becomes our spiritually guided pursuit, the operational intent of a true disciple. As this final apex of His character emerges, *love* makes its mark on our generation, as He works through us to influence the 'neighbours' He places in front of us on a daily basis. Our growing intimate relationship with Jesus builds this structure of His perfect love flowing into us, and performing His activity through us! Praise His Name for such a glorious life!

As my own life edges toward its conclusion, I have seen how this progression took place for me. I look back with fondness at the careful, gentle, patient, kind and loving way the Father has moulded and guided me. He has taken me to places where I have at least *glimpsed* the nature of His love flowing through me to those He has given me loving burdens for. I thank Him for this grace in my life. I love Him so!

POSTURE

It means not seeing how close
you can get to the world
and still be 'acceptable'
to the church,
but seeing how closely
you can get to Jesus.

I am not a servant
of the church.
I am a servant of Christ,
FOR the church.

As you grow in your personal faith and learn to live a biblical culture as a disciple of Jesus, there are a couple of *postures* imperative to
incorporate early on. First, you must adopt the posture of a *citizen of
heaven*, no longer bound by earthly cultural norms, but by unwavering allegiance to God's Kingship over your life. Second, you must carry
yourself in the world with the posture of a *servant*, no longer serving yourself, but serving Christ, your eternal King, in the lives of those
around you.

Citizenship

Living life under the authority and rule of God, by the Word of Christ in
the power of the Spirit is a chosen path. Recounting the exemplary list
of great and faithful 'men of old' in Hebrews 11, verses 13-16 explain,

> *"All these died in faith, without receiving the promises, but*
> *having seen them and having welcomed them from a distance,*

and having confessed that they were strangers and exiles on the earth. For those who say such things make it clear that they are seeking a country of their own. And indeed if they had been thinking of that country from which they went out, they would have had opportunity to return. But as it is, they desire a better country, that is a heavenly one. Therefore God is not ashamed to be called their God; for He has prepared a city for them."

Speaking very personally in Philippians 3, Paul recommends,

"Brethren, join in following my example, and observe those who walk according to the pattern you have in us. For many walk, of whom I often told you, and now tell you even weeping, that they are enemies of the cross of Christ, whose end is destruction, whose god is their appetite, and whose glory is in their shame, who set their minds on earthly things. For our citizenship is in heaven, from which also we eagerly wait for a Savior, the Lord Jesus Christ; who will transform the body of our humble state into conformity with the body of His glory"   Verses 17-21a

As a citizen of heaven you pledge foremost allegiance to the King of heaven, not any earthly rule, nation, tribe or tongue. You live as a human 'in the world, but NOT of the world' (see John 17:11-15). As you travel through this brief life, you "seek first His kingdom" and life's true needs "shall be added to you" (Matthew 6:33). You see the world not for what you can get from it, but for what you can feed into it. Your hands find purposeful, helpful things to do. You work 'that you might have something to share with those in need' (Ephesians 4:28).

Inwardly, the Kingdom life sets all aspirations, all delights, and all devotion toward the King of all Kings as you learn to make Him your Lord. It is a daily walk as a citizen of heaven that makes God's activities the priority and joy of your life to participate in. It sees every person before you as a living treasure of God, in need of healing, restoration and reconciliation with God. It means not walking around concerned about being appealing, successful, handsome, or beautiful toward other humans, but walking in the humble confidence of resurrection power, seeking to enhance others by the inward beauty of Christ, whom you represent. It means representing the authority of Christ, offering the pure love of God and the light of salvation to all who cross your path.

Outwardly, the Kingdom life is meant to imitate the life of Christ in such a manner that people are drawn to God by the example of your lifestyle, not repelled by the hypocrisy of it. It means not giving off conflicting messages that mix worldliness with heavenliness. It means not seeing how close you can get to the world and still be *acceptable* to the church, but seeing how closely you can get to Jesus. It means dying to self and walking alive to Christ, "so that in the thing in which they slander you as evildoers, they may on account of your good deeds, as they observe *them*, glorify God' (see 1 Peter 2:9-12).

You see, "Every good thing bestowed and every perfect gift is from above, coming down from the Father of lights" (James 1:17a). That is, everything that is right, that is best for you, and best for those around you, initiates with God, and not mankind. Every influence for good has its starting point in heaven and is accessible to the citizen of heaven.

We must live out the Kingdom for all of mankind without preference to race, creed, colour, nationality, tribe or tongue. Have you ever noticed that American presidents often declare, "God bless America", but never go beyond that to 'God bless the *world*'? It is this kind of self-focus that hinders true justice and liberty FOR ALL.

Certainly we can be proud of the country we reside in, but pledging allegiance to one country over all others necessarily shifts our focus from God's will for the globe, to the self-focused will of a marred human culture, and we lose His greater perspective of true global needs.

God rises up and takes down nations to accomplish His deep purposes, understood by Him alone. We are thus called to pledge our allegiance to heaven, stand upon the Word of God, which "abides forever" (1 Peter 1:25) and let Him lead us within this world.

For the Kingdom to flourish, through the ministry and example of His *citizens*, we must each commit under the influence of the Spirit to become 'good soil' (see Matthew 13:23) for the message of Christ to be represented through. We carry the good news of the Gospel in our mortal frames; the 'hope of the nations', the 'light of the world', the message of salvation and reconciliation back to the relationship we were all meant to have with our Creator!

The Kingdom life is ONLY plausible and possible through a surrendered and sacrificial life that is "transformed by the renewing of your mind" (Romans 12:2) and 'conformed to His image' (Romans 8:29), 'walking by the Spirit and not by the desire of the flesh' (Galatians 5:16). The Kingdom life CAN be lived out by sinners 'saved by grace' (Ephesians 2:5), not in perfection, but by the kind of devotion that daily exhibits faith in His ways as the best way, the only way and living out 'the narrow path that leads to life' (Matthew 7:14). It means starting every day in the palace of His presence, drawing on Him for the strength to be an ambassador of His kingdom in the world, and for the determination to be His servant, ready for any sacrificial assignment He commands.

Servanthood

The second posture needed for living a biblical culture in the world is that of a 'servant'. Consider this passage:

> *"And they came to Capernaum; and when He [Jesus] was in the house, He began to question them [the disciples], "What were you discussing on the way?" But they kept silent, for on the way they had discussed with one another which of them was*

the greatest. And sitting down, He called the twelve and said to them, "If anyone wants to be first, he shall be last of all, and servant of all."   Mark 9:33-35

For so many in the church, our lifestyles need to be turned on their heads, for we act, pray, and live like He is OUR servant... 'God give me a car', 'make it sunny today', 'give me financial prosperity'. What if He wants you to minister to a person on the bus route... why would you spoil that by driving a car? What if He wants to provide rain for the garden of your neighbour... why would you command the sun to shine for your 'garage sale'? And what if He asks you to "go *and* sell your possessions and give to *the* poor, and you shall have treasure in heaven; and come, follow Me" (Matthew 19:21b)?

Of course, taking on the posture of a servant doesn't mean quitting your job and sitting around waiting for God to tell you to do something for Him. If you think of the analogy of a slave to his master, the slave goes about doing the prescribed generic duties to please his master, but when the master calls, he stops what he is doing, and does the specific things that serve the master's purposes, not his own. We are called to be 'bond-servants' to our Master, Jesus! Jesus Himself specifically proclaimed,

"whoever wishes to become great among you shall be your servant, and whoever wishes to be first among you shall be your slave; just as the Son of Man did not come to be served, but to serve, and to give His life a ransom for many."
Matthew 20:26b-28

Now let me be clear, a 'servant of all' does not mean letting others rule over you, commanding you to do what they want you to do for them. I remember having to explain once to a congregation, 'Fire me whenever you like, but I am not a servant of the church; I am a servant of Christ FOR the church'. As a citizen of heaven and a bond-servant in the palace of King Jesus, I voluntarily bind myself to His Kingship over me, and devote my life to serving His wishes, 'for the good of others'. My life is no longer my own, for I have been 'bought with a price'. Peter described us as

"A CHOSEN RACE, A royal PRIESTHOOD, A HOLY NATION, A PEOPLE FOR God's OWN POSSESSION, that you may proclaim the excellencies of Him who has called you out of darkness into His marvellous light;"   *1 Peter 2:9*

The great and magnificent beauty of serving our Heavenly King is that we get to enjoy all the benefits of the royal palace, while we herald His 'good news' to the nations! Whatever we ask in His Name (according to His will) we receive (see 1 John 3:21-22)! We have the benefit of the protection of His 'fortress' (2 Samuel 22:2) as our place of refuge! All of His 'armour' is available for us to wage spiritual warfare with the enemy of our soul (see Ephesians 6:11-17), and we obtain the joys of His eternal kingdom. For

"did not God choose the poor of this world to be rich in faith and heirs of the kingdom which He promised to those who love Him?"   *James 2:5*

Jesus modeled a high standard for us to imitate as servants of God; "I do nothing on My own initiative, but I speak these things as the Father taught Me" (John 8:28). John 5:30 cites,

"I can do nothing on My own initiative. As I hear, I judge; and My judgment is just, because I do not seek My own will, but the will of Him who sent Me."

John 12:49 adds:

"For I did not speak on My own initiative, but the Father Himself who sent Me has given Me commandment, what to say, and what to speak." John 14:10: "Do you not believe that I am in the Father, and the Father is in Me? The words that I say to you I do not speak on My own initiative, but the Father abiding in Me does His works."

As you live to do the unique ministry God has provided you, make sure you retain the posture of servitude, being responsive to His Word and attuned to His Voice, so that when He gives a command, a prompting, or a nudge to speak or lend a hand, you obey!

Many question what the 'will of God' is for them, but 1 Thessalonians 5:16-18 makes it clear: "Rejoice always; pray without ceasing; in everything give thanks; for this is God's will for you in Christ Jesus." Developing this kind of lifestyle will help you follow the Lord's initiatives as you serve Him faithfully as a citizen of heaven.

I could not be more joyful and at peace, than resting in the truth and love of God, and walking with Him ever before me, behind me, in me and all around me. Jesus has been my greatest strength, my deepest love and the joy of my salvation. I most gladly continue in devotion to serve His Kingdom!

[DOING]

Up to this point in the book most of the focus has been on 'BEING'. I have tried to share my heart and thoughts concerning the paramount value of intimately and completely falling in love with God.

For each individual, as well as the collective 'Church' of His people, we are pictured as a Bride, with Christ as the Groom, preparing for the 'marriage feast' at the end of this world's dark conclusion (see Matthew 22:1-14; Revelation 19:7-9). Our relationship with Him is to mirror a marriage commitment of lifetime love and singular devotion. As intimacy with our Creator deepens, the whole agenda of our life should begin to revolve around serving His desires, seeking His will and enjoying His Presence.

Now I would like to turn to some thoughts about 'DOING'. Our vertical love relationship, of course, as set out in Scripture, is the *greatest commandment*;

"YOU SHALL LOVE THE LORD YOUR GOD WITH ALL YOUR HEART, AND WITH ALL YOUR SOUL, AND WITH ALL YOUR MIND, AND WITH ALL YOUR STRENGTH."   *Mark 12:30*

Loving Him in this all-encompassing way necessarily propels us to *loving others* He equally cares about. Jesus follows up this greatest commandment with a second command, 'like the first',

"You shall LOVE YOUR NEIGHBOUR AS YOURSELF."

Mark 12:31

This mandate sets us apart upon a new horizontal path of sacrificial other-centered living for the balance of our earthly life, as outlined in what many call the *Great Commission*, to "Go therefore and make disciples of all the nations" (Matthew 28:19a).

DISCIPLESHIP

There's no better life
than having a
'God story' every day;
something He has
done for you
or through you,
or something you have
observed Him do!

Now growth in and of itself may greatly help your own life, by bringing you deep personal meaning and satisfaction from God's unconditional love and sense of tremendous worth toward you. But that is only part of God's intention for bestowing salvation upon your life.

"Jesus came into Galilee, preaching the gospel of God, and saying,
"The time is fulfilled, and the kingdom of God is at hand; repent
and believe in the gospel." And as He was going along by the
Sea of Galilee, He saw Simon and Andrew, the brother of Simon,
casting a net in the sea; for they were fishermen. And Jesus said
to them, "Follow Me, and I will make you become fishers of men."
And they immediately left the nets and followed Him."
Mark 1:14b-18

A disciple is more than a repentant believer in the gospel. A disciple is one who responds to God's call, and follows Jesus into an *other-centered* life. Living a biblical culture as a disciple of Christ is so challenging that Jesus warned us to first 'count the cost' (Luke 14:28-30), so we would not fall short and be labelled a hypocrite.

In this same passage Jesus lists three actual prerequisites for discipleship (I outlined them earlier, in the section about *Lordship*, but they bear repeating here.). The first is placing greatest value upon our relationship with Him, over and above all human relationships, even cherished family members! "If anyone comes to Me, and does not hate his own father and mother and wife and children and brothers and sisters, yes and even his own life, he cannot be My disciple" (verse 26).

Second is sacrificially giving up our own worldly plans in lieu of accepting His greater purposes for our life. "Whoever does not carry His own cross and come after Me cannot be My disciple" (verse 27). And third, we must relinquish to Him full charge over all our possessions, so they do not entangle us with worldly priorities, or even distract us from full devotion to Him. "So therefore, no one of you can be My disciple who does not give up all his own possessions" (verse 33).

He follows these conditions with a sobering warning against preoccupation with earthly cultural pursuits, using the analogy of salt.

"Therefore, salt is good; but if even salt has become tasteless, with what will it be seasoned? It is useless either for the soil or for the manure pile; it is thrown out. He who has ears to hear, let him hear."   Verses 34-35

A disciple can no longer adopt the values of the prevailing human culture. There is really no point in being a disciple, if you are not willing and able to demonstrate a better and more compelling path for living to this darkening world.

Jesus condenses the conditions; "If anyone wishes to come after Me, let him deny himself, and take up his cross, and follow Me" (Mark 8:34). One of the most profound and astonishing remarks from Jesus is His allusion to the image of *carrying your cross*, before He was even nailed upon it! In fact, He already knew the cross lay ahead, yet His whole earthly existence would be one of self-sacrifice, for the eternal benefit of others. He was prepared to die a horrific death on a cross for others!

As a 12 year old boy, Jesus was 'about His Father's business' (Luke 2:49). There was no evidence of self-focused living, even then, before He reached his teens years!

Later in ministry, when He was saddened by the news of John's beheading, He withdrew "in a boat, to a lonely place by Himself" (Matthew 14:13). But "when He went ashore, He saw a great multitude, and felt compassion for them, and healed their sick" (verse 14). In the darkest of hours, His love and commitment for others never wavered. Even at the end, crucified on that cross, He exclaimed, "Father forgive them, for they do not know what they are doing" (Luke 23:34a). This is the mark of a true disciple.

"No soldier in active service entangles himself in the affairs of everyday life, so that he may please the one who enlisted him as a soldier."   2 Timothy 2:4

The life of a disciple is sacrificial by its very nature, since it is a conscious denial of the ways of the surrounding culture, the desires of our own sinful human flesh and the deceptive and destructive lures of the devil and his legion of fallen angels.

Jesus was in the midst of a detailed teaching to His new disciples when He declared,

"Enter by the narrow gate; for the gate is wide, and the way is broad that leads to destruction, and many are those who enter by it. For the gate is small, and the way is narrow that leads to life, and few are those who find it."   Matthew 7:13-14

I have referred to this passage a number of times already. Many assume the broad way is the roadway of non-believers and the narrow path is for those who call themselves Christians. But actually, many 'believers' are going down the highway to spiritual apathy, lifelessness and even destruction. Jesus goes on to illustrate this, speaking of false prophets within the ranks of the church. He then continues in Matthew 7:24-27 to highlight two foundations among Christians; that of a house built upon rock, and another built upon shifting sand, which symbolically cannot weather the spiritual storms and attacks that come to bear upon the Church of God's people. The determining factor that distinguishes a disciple from a mere assenting 'believer' is *obedience*!

"Therefore everyone who hears these words of Mine, and acts upon them, may be compared to a wise man, who built his house upon the rock [a central image of Jesus as the rock, and Cornerstone of our living faith]. "   *Matthew 7:24*

Let me illustrate what this 'choice' looks like. Picture yourself as an orphan, with no family to love you. Imagine a father comes alongside you and invites you into their family. You are, of course, skeptical at first, silently wondering what the 'catch' is. The Father, understanding your hesitancy simply says, "Why don't you just come and see my house. Take a look around it, and see if our family is one you would like to join."

Upon viewing the house and the family, you begin to experience the warmth and genuine nature of their love. You come to believe that becoming a part of this family will be so much better than the secret loneliness and longings you have had to deal with, especially in the dark hours of the night. So you decide to join this loving family and intertwine your life with theirs. At this point the Father lays out what it will cost you to live your life as they do. You will need to lay aside your old life and take up a brand new life together with them.

Now at this point in the story one of four things will occur. They are recounted in the parable of the sower. Matthew 13:18-23 details,

Hear then the parable of the sower. "When anyone hears the word of the kingdom, and does not understand it, the evil one comes and snatches away what has been sown in his heart. This is the one on whom seed was sown beside the road. "And the one on whom seed was sown on the rocky places, this is the man who hears the word, and immediately receives it with joy; yet he has no firm root in himself, but is only temporary, and when affliction or persecution arises because of the word, immediately he falls away. "And the one on whom seed was sown among the thorns, this is the man who hears the word, and the worry of the world, and the deceitfulness of riches choke the word, and it becomes unfruitful. "And the one on whom seed was sown on the good soil, this is the man who hears the word and understands it; who indeed bears fruit and brings forth, some a hundredfold, some sixty, and some thirty."

As you begin living with your new family, you may simply not 'get' how the new family benefits you, and go off on your own again. You may neglect becoming rooted in the life and values of the family, and run, when things get tough. You may ignore the security and eternal nature of your new family, letting the worries and values that plagued you before, encroach again into your life. Or, you might accept your new family joyfully, take on their wonderful values and beliefs, and begin to encourage other orphans into the home of your adopted family.

For this process to be fully appreciated and enjoyed, salvation must turn to belief and then belief into discipleship. Jesus commands us to 'go and make other disciples' (Matthew 28:19a). He exemplified this process using three basic steps. The first was a friendly invitation to 'come and see' where He was staying (John 1:39). The next stage of invitation, "follow Me" (John 1:43) involved walking with Him and observing Him in ministry. This was followed by the greater commitment to participate with Him in ministry, to 'be with Me' (John 12:26). In this manner Jesus Himself encouraged new believers to keep progressing with Him in ministry, by increasing in personal intimacy and devotion toward Him.

Many never get to experience the deep joy that comes from this *denying of self* and *living for Christ*. To 'take up one's cross and follow Christ' is so much more rewarding than merely believing He is who He claims to be, singing praises to Him and listening to endless sermons about Him. Discipleship fords the depths of one's soul to root out what is not of Him. It aims to consistently give up the temporary nature of society's cultural values for the greater eternal pleasures of intimacy with the Creator, His one and only Son, and the Spirit who resides in you to comfort, guide, strengthen and evoke His love through your sacrificial life!

This involves a whole new culture of seeing the world through God's eyes and being daily available to participate in His activity and promptings as you go about living in the world, 'but not of the world' (John 15:19).

I tell people all the time; "There's no better life than having a 'God story' every day"; something He has done for you or through you, or something you have observed Him do!

When I would first start pastoring a church family, I always included a 'testimony time' during the Sunday service. I wanted to instil in the congregation early on, the importance of every member participating in God's activities through the week. Then they could passionately share those 'God stories' when we gathered, to encourage each other. Hebrews 10:24 directs us to "consider how to stimulate one another to love and good deeds."

I remember distinctly in one of these churches opening it up for the first time. Initially no one spoke, then after an exceedingly long silence, one person around 60 years of age reluctantly got up and shared something that God had done through him when he was 17. That was one of the saddest moments of pastoring for me. While I was thrilled that God had used him, I thought to myself, "Has no one here had a more recent experience of being part of the activity of God?"

Brothers and sisters, we ought to be able to share the joy of proclaiming how God has used us on any given day. We were created to be disciples of Jesus, *followers* of His teachings and *participants* with His ongoing will on earth. We are *citizens of heaven*, and *fishers of men*, moving about this world, helping to accomplish His will in the lives of those He loves all around us. If you step out in this way, I can assure you; you will not be disappointed!

RELATIONSHIPS

The process of becoming
a disciple takes us
from looking FOR love,
to looking TO love;
and from longing FOR worth,
to proclaiming HIS worth!

We were built for relationship.

From the very outset with Adam in Genesis 2:18, God, Himself a Trinity of relational Persons, declared, "It is not good for the man to be alone" and then created Eve to be with him. Since we are made in the image of God, the animals and other created beings are not intended to fully occupy that role (see Genesis 2:20). Near the end of the Bible, in 1 John 1:3, John announces:

> *"what we have seen and heard we proclaim to you also, that you also may have fellowship with us; and indeed our fellowship is with the Father, and with His Son Jesus Christ."*

From the very beginning of humanity to the gates of glory, we are meant to have biblically cultural fellowship with one another, and with the triune God. So how do these relationships integrate together?

I believe as you make the necessary transition from salvation to Lordship, placing priority on living out a biblical culture, at least two things will radically shift in the arena of your relationships. I noted earlier that the two relational things mankind lost in the garden through original sin, which can only be fully restored by God, are *unconditional love* and *self-worth*.

Concerning unconditional love, I observe that the process of becoming a disciple takes us from 'looking FOR love' to a new position of 'looking TO love'. Our relationships are necessarily flawed while in pursuit of someone to love us unconditionally. We are all fallen beings and thus unable to provide or receive this complete purity of love with another human. So, we settle for what we can get. It may be as desperate as a one night stand, thinking 'at least they like me enough to pick me to spend the night with'. It may be much healthier, within a lifelong marriage, based upon what he does for her and what she does for him. But the real prize is receiving that life transforming relationship with God, and experiencing His uniquely unconditional love as it was originally extended before sin separated us from Him.

As intimacy with God increases and you get to know His completely satisfying love, you are then truly set free from the bondage of that insatiable quest to be loved. You now become free to have God extend His love through you, to others. The joy unspeakable that percolates within a disciple living out a biblical culture provides the ability to share the love of God with others in a compelling manner. Few can resist the ongoing offer of pure love.

People outside the faith need to hear what is wonderful about God in our lives. Within His own family, the Church, we are meant to enjoy unconditional love among the members, as we allow Him to demonstrate His love through us to one another. John 13:35 boldly asserts, "By this all men will know that you are My disciples, if you have love for one another." Galatians 6:10 adds, "let us do good to all men, and especially to those who are of the household of the faith." It is my prayer that His love will be *enough* for you, so that every human relationship can be seen as a bonus, and fostered in an appropriate and wonderful manner.

Similarly with 'self-worth', He takes us from 'longing FOR worth' to 'proclaiming HIS worth!' How you view your *worth* can either be one of the most debilitating barriers to joy-filled living, or the greatest catalyst for creating the deepest of relationships with others. How you perceive yourself amongst your peers is a major factor in how relationships form or break apart. We all long for those who will *value* us. A lack of personal worth can drive a person to the harmful overemphasis of trying to prove themselves.

For example, a bike gang candidate may shoot another human being, just to be accepted into membership. Another may never reach their potential due to a false sense of unworthiness. Many people succumb to being devalued by cultures who demand success, beauty in appearance, high intelligence, wit, charm and the like.

But once you discover, and come to really comprehend the supreme value God places upon your soul and personhood, your self-worth can heal from the various kinds of abuse you may have suffered in your life. Knowing your value to Him can give you confidence to be in His Presence again, and to 'proclaim HIS worth' to others!

His complete value of you is not based upon what your talents, appearance or accomplishments are, but solely on His creation of you as your heavenly Father! To me, it means He valued me enough that He uniquely and specifically designed and established me. This enables me to uniquely join with Him in certain aspects of His activity on earth, to help produce heavenly glory. He created me to enjoy Him forever! He valued me enough to give up His only Son on the cross for my restoration back to Himself, and He values my fellowship in His service.

Through my life, since my conversion experience at the age of fifteen, there has not been a time when I have doubted His love for me, or my worth to Him. They helped me through the balance of my teen years by no longer needing to respond to the pressure of peers by conforming to their ways. In fact, my very confidence of faith gained me a new respect within my high school culture. They helped me through the early years of leadership to overcome feelings of inadequacy and fear of failure. They helped me through pastoring four congregations to remain confident in His effective use of my gifts during times of persecution. They continue to help me thrive today while ministering in a culture where I am in the minority among two oft times opposing larger cultures. I pray you too will know the depth of His love toward you, and His value of you, so you can rise above relational barriers and permit His love to effectively emanate from you to others.

SEXUALITY

Many in the world see the Bible
as the enemy of sexuality,
when it is, in fact,
the only true standard.

Coming together in sexual union
and becoming 'one flesh'
is meant to be the
'climax' of the story,
not the introduction.

Before I share any thoughts concerning marriage and family, I want to address the general issue of sexuality. It is a delicate subject but I feel it needs to be talked about more readily and openly; for God created us as sexual beings. Sexual intimacy and sexual union play a role in all of our lives. We are all given strong sexual *urges* at the commencement of our teen years. But if we can grasp that our deepest longing is not for sex, but for unconditional love and a sense of self-worth, found ONLY in God, then sexual engagement would fall into a healthy place and serve its intended role in our lives.

Many in the world see the Bible as the *enemy* of sexuality, when it is in fact the only true standard, guiding us to its beautiful unfolding in marriage, and guarding us from all the destructive consequences of sexual intimacy outside of marriage.

Living a biblical culture is especially important when it comes to our sexuality. The Bible even highlights a separate category for its improper use.

"Every other sin that a man commits is outside the body, but the immoral man sins against his own body. Or do you not know that your body is a temple of the Holy Spirit who is in you, whom you have from God, and that you are not your own? For you have been bought with a price: therefore glorify God in your body."
1 Corinthians 6:18-20

How is it possible to *glorify God* with your sexuality, except by following the very standards He sets, and the parameters He places upon it for your good? The great danger of following any human cultural standard is the manner in which it shifts over time. What is *wrong* for one generation becomes *right* for the next. 'Immorality' by its very definition as 'behaviours and actions outside the moral standards of society', demonstrates shifting societal norms as an insufficient source of reliance.

The entire catalogue of thoughts in this book are based on the premise that human cultures are all tainted by various sins and thus provide an unreliable foundation for standards of conduct and living. Only a life built upon the solid, unchanging foundation of biblical truth will provide the freedom we need from the bondage of sin and its devastating consequences.

So please bear with me as I humbly unfold some thoughts which have helped me navigate my own life as it pertains to sexuality.

Heterosexuality

The Bible clearly denies engagement in both fornication and adultery (see Matthew 15:18-20; Romans 13:9; Hebrews 13:4). Fornication is basically sexual intercourse between any two unmarried people. Similarly, adultery is voluntary (as opposed to forced) sexual intercourse between a married person and another not their spouse. So the only option left for sexual union in God's economy is within the confines of marriage; between one man and one woman (Genesis 2:21-25; Ephesians 5:31-33).

God designed our bodies such that a man only 'fits' into a woman, thereby excluding sexual intimacy with another of the same sex. But the deeper reason for a disciple not to marry within the same sex is that it taints the picture God intends marriage to signify between Christ (the Groom) and His Church (the bride). "This mystery is great; but I am speaking with reference to Christ and the church" (Ephesians 5:32). If you are *most* in love with God, you will adhere to this, even if it becomes sacrificial to do so.

In the dating process leading up to marriage, many scoff at *abstinence* with brash comments like, "You've got to kick the tires before you buy the car", or, "It's better to live together for a while and see if we are compatible." Just slow down and take a moment to let the shallowness of those lines of thinking settle in.

How sad to jump ahead sexually and miss the enormous privilege of joining as one flesh with the one you have just committed the rest of your life to before God. And how frivolous to ignore God's leading in your life toward the spouse He has uniquely designed to complement and complete you. In your selfishness and ignorance, you may cry 'incompatible' before He has used each of you to refine the other from your sinful ways to a place of great compatibility, freedom and love!

When speaking to youth gatherings on this issue, I often get one of the guys to come to the front and eat a chocolate bar. I ask him if he enjoyed it, to the inevitable reply, "Absolutely!" After a pause, I drop the empty wrapper out of my hand to the floor and explain, "This is what you have just done to the girl you 'enjoyed' yourself with." By selfishly engaging your sexual *urges*, she has now been emptied of some of her self-worth and lost some sense of true love. She will now forever see herself more as a *useful body*, than a *truly treasured soul*.

1 Thessalonians 5:21-23 urges,

"But examine everything carefully; hold fast to that which is good; abstain from every form of evil. Now may the God of peace Himself sanctify you entirely; and may your spirit and soul and body be preserved complete, without blame at the coming of our Lord Jesus Christ."

As we learn to trust Christ to guide our lives, He will make the right choice for us, and give us the strength, conviction and perseverance to reserve our sexual pleasures for that one and only precious soul we will journey through life with, for as long as God gives us breath together!

Coming together in sexual union and becoming 'one flesh' is meant to be the climax of the story, not the introduction. Regardless of the legal ceremony, it is the 'actual' transition from acquaintance, friendship and engagement, to a life commitment in marriage that culminates in a sexual union.

Many, even in the church see the purpose of sexual union to be for procreation, and pleasure. I disagree. I see the *urges* as given by God to ensure 'marriage' occurs, and then procreation and pleasure will have their special place within that proper context. Pleasure will be heightened as we take the time and loving care to provide stimulation for our spouse first and foremost! The beauty of intimacy is largely lost when either one comes focused solely to gratify their own flesh, and not primarily their spouse's satisfaction. Children become a natural 'gift' from that sexual union in marriage, not an unintended by-product of sex outside of marriage.

God used the Apostle Paul to give us much information in 1 Corinthians 6 and 7 about sexuality and its intended role in devotion to living a biblical culture. For example, Paul actually recommends that we remain single in order to offer full devotion to the Lord:

"One who is unmarried is concerned about the things of the Lord, how he may please the Lord; but one who is married is concerned about the things of the world, how he may please his wife, and his interests are divided." 1 Corinthians 7:32b-34;

likewise the women also. Earlier in the chapter he states,

"But I say to the unmarried and to widows that it is good for them if they remain even as I. But if they do not have self-control, let them marry; for it is better to marry than to burn." 1 Corinthians 7:8-9

This statement has been key to my understanding of sexual purity outside of marriage. It says, 'better to marry than burn'. It does not say better to have a one night stand, sleep with a girlfriend/boyfriend, or masturbate than to burn. The only proper remedy given for an inability to control sexual urges is to 'marry'.

So what do we do with these strong God-given sexual urges? Let me first speak to why God gave us these 'urges' at such a young age? I believe the better question to ask is "Why do so many cultures delay marriage until later in life?" In Jesus' day marriages were permitted at the age of 12 for girls and 14 for boys. They simply 'got their own tent', so to speak, and continued under the umbrella of the family until they were older.

So many cultures foster the completion of education and the acquiring of a career prior to marriage, primarily for economic reasons. In essence, the culture has it wrong, not God. He could have given the onset of sexual desire at 30 or 50 years of age. Why so early?

Once again I believe the answer lies right back in Genesis with Adam and Eve. "Then the Lord God said, "It is not good for the man to be alone; I will make him a helper suitable for him (Genesis 2:18)".

Two things I see here. First, if it is not good for man to be alone, why do we wait into our late twenties or early thirties to marry, when we have become so self-sufficient on our own that the companionship of marriage seems less desirable? We are meant to have a *helper*, and the teen years are the very season we begin moving out from under our family's values, and commence shaping our own. How marvellous of God to permit us to marry so soon, and have that helper alongside as we develop our own deep loving relationship with the Triune God.

Second, God made a helper 'suitable'. If God created someone *suitable* for you, why would you choose to wait an extra ten or fifteen years to have them by your side to truly *complete* you? If your weaker areas are their strengths and their weaknesses your strengths, why delay the 'wholeness' of married living as one, provided by God for your enhancement?

Here in Honduras many boys and girls come together and have babies at twelve years of age or shortly thereafter. A long period of excruciating abstinence is not part of their experience. Unfortunately, in Caribbean culture, marriage is not seen as a necessary part of that equation and so most homes lack a father in the raising of these precious children, to their great detriment, in most cases.

My point is that earlier marriages will help alleviate many of the devastating consequences of sexual promiscuity, and studies have shown that early marriages have a much lower rate of divorce.

But for those cultures unwilling or unable to bend to this God-designed intention of teenage marriage, how do we handle these strong sexual urges *in the meantime,* until a later marriage?

Here are three things that helped guard me against giving in to sexual urges until marriage. First, and foremost, love God sufficiently.

"How can a young man keep his way pure? by keeping it according to Thy word. With all my heart I have sought Thee; do

*not let me wander from Thy commandments. Thy word I have
treasured in my heart, that I may not sin against Thee."*
Psalm 119:9-11

Only by maintaining enough incentive from your intimate love of
the Father, will you have sufficient abhorrence of impure sexual sin to
abstain.

Still vivid are my own recollections of the deep remorse I felt from
the few girls I touched inappropriately as a new young Christian. Afterward, it seemed my life with God was over and He would never again
use me for His Kingdom. I also recognized some of the negative effect
it had on those wonderful Christian girls, and my heart still sinks over
the results of my lack of control. It was only by my growing love for Jesus and God's great mercy that I never went further, and was later able
to give myself to my wife alone!

A second factor, which assisted me in this regard, was to become
fully engaged in spiritual ministry at an early age, and remain so. Concentrate on pleasing the Lord in the light of day, rather than pleasing
yourself in the hours of darkness. Romans 13 offers,

*"Let us therefore lay aside the deeds of darkness and put on
the armor of light. Let us behave properly as in the day, not
in carousing and drunkenness, not in sexual promiscuity and
sensuality, not in strife and jealousy. But put on the Lord Jesus
Christ, and make no provision for the flesh in regard to its
lusts."*   *Verses 12b-14*

1 Corinthians 15:33 insightfully adds,

"Do not be deceived: bad company corrupts good morals."

In speaking about being a 'workman' for Christ, Paul writes,

"Now flee from youthful lusts, and pursue righteousness, faith,
love and peace, with those who call on the Lord from a pure
heart"   *2 Timothy 2:22*

Within a few weeks of accepting Christ, God graciously helped surround me with Christian peers, similarly bent on following Jesus. As we learned of Christ together, many of our school friends began coming to us for advice, inquiring about our faith and joining hands with Christ themselves. It was a time that could have been destroyed by self-seeking momentary lustful pleasures. Instead, it launched us ahead to make disciples around the globe. Most of my fellow Christians from those first days remain highly involved in Christian ministry today.

Now a third area of real helpfulness here is simply for each gender to help the other out by dressing more modestly, and treating each other more respectfully for the sake of the Kingdom. Guys are made to be attracted to a woman's physique. That is good and from God. The attraction ensures marriage, and then procreation throughout the generations.

The problem lies in the improper response to the attraction. It is the responsibility of the young men to exhibit self-control. But ladies, you can sure help us out in this regard. Men are strongly stimulated by lines and curves. The more you display these features, the more difficult it is for the guys to behave properly around you.

I understand there are deep issues acting against this recommendation. Women want to be liked and noticed, and early on discover their figure can assist them in this regard. This all stems from those two primary desires for unconditional love and self-worth. Only if a girl finds these sufficiently from her heavenly Father, will she not find it necessary to *acquire* them from guys, using her figure as a tool.

If only you will trust God that through expending your energies serving Him, He will bring someone *suitable* for you to come alongside. You do not need to overly expose your outer beauty to accomplish this.

I often tell young girls we are mentoring, "Wait for a guy who falls in love with your inside more than your outside!" When you unduly display your physique, you are bound to accomplish one of two things, or both. First, you will attract those who just want your outside, with sometimes devastating results. Second, you may cause some of the good guys to stumble, unable to withstand their attraction to your *display*. If you end up marrying a guy who is primarily attracted to your outside, there is a high probability he will be attracted to someone else's outside, even after marriage. So why dress against the kind of love you really want deep down in your heart? You must take seriously the biblical admonition,

> *"do you not know that your body is a temple of the Holy Spirit who is in you, whom you have from God, and that you are not your own? For you have been bought with a price; therefore glorify God in your body."*   *1 Corinthians 6:19-20*

Jesus spilled his blood to redeem you back to Himself, for your eternal benefit. How can you in return so frivolously accentuate your figure for your own glory, rather than saving it for your husband, and bring glory to God? I am sometimes tempted to say to some of the island girls, "Your breasts are given to you for two reasons… your babies and your husband… so why are you showing them to me?" Now I may seem harsh here, but it puzzles me why girls get so offended by being asked to help their brothers in Christ in this sacrificial way.

Now I say to the boys in similar fashion: make a similar sacrifice for your sisters in Christ. Don't pray on a woman's vulnerable desire for love, companionship and 'worth', just to achieve a fleeting moment of self-gratification. One of the qualities of love, listed in 1 Corinthians 13 is that "love does not seek its own" (verse 5b). Our relationships with females must remain focused on *their* good, and not our own. What will help my sister become closer to our Father? How can I foster her devotion to Jesus? I know how utterly distracting it can be, when they are tightly or openly dressed, but as Paul declared, "I buffet my body and make it my slave, lest possibly, after I have preached to others, I myself should be disqualified" (1 Corinthians 9:27).

One strategy I have found effective with particularly beautiful women, is to simply get to know them better. From a distance, there is the danger of lingering thoughts and desires. But by delving into what their inner fears, aspirations and challenges are, it helps you begin to care more about *their* needs, than your own. If you are willing to explore the character and personality of a woman, you will be better enabled to withstand your sexual passions toward her, and endure your virginity until marriage.

I know I am speaking against a raging river in the opposite direction here (there are now shamefully over a billion pornographic sites on the internet), but I pray it helps some of you change your ways and behaviours to further the activities of God, and not quench His Spirit for momentary pleasures.

1 Peter 2:11 reads, "Beloved, I urge you as aliens and strangers to abstain from fleshly lusts, which wage war against the soul." Sexuality continues to be a great tool of the enemy to devour followers of Christ. I highly recommend both sexes take the time for a careful reading of Proverbs 7. For the ladies, be warned not to take on any of these dreadful characteristics and actions of an adulteress, even in a teasing manner. You have no idea how difficult it is on the guys you do this to. Men,

take special heed not to be 'naïve' and 'lacking sense' (verse 7) enough to follow your lustful thoughts to the window of a girl at night! You may end up like an 'ox led to the slaughter' (verse 22).

For both genders, you have a better chance of a long lasting marriage and happiness if you capture the attention of the kind of person who is, yes, attracted to your outside, but primarily falls in love with your inside, your personality, your 'inner soul'. Downplaying sensual teasing and sexual appearance should characterize a man or woman of God trying to live out a biblical culture in these darkening days.

Homosexuality

Now for those who face strong attraction to others of the same sex, let me say I have great sympathy for you. However, I have a similar lack of tolerance for those who engage their *urges* sexually. If sexual intimacy is biblically reserved for marriage, then it is forbidden outside of marriage regardless of the object of those urges.

Whether same sex attraction is by birth or by choice is a conversational argument I hear a lot these days. Can one help being sexually attracted to another of their gender or not? Well, if homosexuality is by birth, then it would be condoned by God. But the Bible does not condone it, so God must have another explanation for why this kind of attraction occurs. I hold that there is both a cultural and a spiritual reason for this tendency.

Spiritually, in Romans 1, a biblical explanation is carefully and thoroughly laid out for us. Romans 1:18-32 outlines some of the unbiblical consequences of ungodliness, and unrighteousness through unbelief; one being the lustfulness and sexual part of same gender attraction.

A biblical culture acknowledges the clear evidence of Creator God, known inside each of us, since "His invisible attributes, His eternal power and divine nature, have been clearly seen, being understood through what has been made" (verse20). No one living on this awesome planet has any legitimate excuse for denying God's existence.

When men choose not to honour God or thank Him for their life and they "suppress the truth in unrighteousness" (verse 18), it continues, "their foolish heart [becomes] darkened" (verse 21). This is a direct consequence of their suppression of truth about God (verse18). Once someone *prefers* their own human ways over the eternal Design, God sadly gives them over "in the lusts of their hearts to impurity, that their bodies might be dishonoured among them" (verse 24).

In the case of homosexual behaviour, the result is that "they exchanged the truth of God for a lie, and worshiped and served the creature rather than the Creator" (verse 25). In other words, when we choose to prioritise the passions of man above the designs of the living God, some are awarded the consequences that

"God gave them over to degrading passions; for their women exchanged the natural function for that which is unnatural, and in the same way also the men abandoned the natural function of the woman and burned in their desire toward one another, men with men committing indecent acts and receiving in their own persons the due penalty of their error."   *Verses 26-27*

Further consequences included a "depraved mind, to do those things which are not proper" (verse 28b). The outcome of this is, "being filled with all unrighteousness, wickedness, greed, evil; full of envy, murder strife, deceit, malice" (verse 29), and a host of other negative characteristics found in any societal culture... all because of a refusal to "acknowledge God" (verse 28).

I have also observed a social reason, based on confusing messages given in many cultures. My crude version of it goes like this. Everyone is born with a combination of their father's 'stuff' and their mother's 'stuff'. If the DNA comprises almost the same amount, then a boy would have more feminine characteristics and a woman would display more masculine tendencies. Conversely, if most of the DNA is male then the man would exhibit very masculine traits, while a woman with mostly female DNA would demonstrate the opposite.

Since God creates us all uniquely, a biblical culture would accept that there are no *better* or *worse* standards amongst His people, for all are created just as they are meant to be, to uniquely contribute to the surrounding community.

The difficulty lays in the *cultural* confusion which translates into the minds of young impressionable children, who are not properly guided to navigate the growing affections they become aware of as 'healthy and normal'.

Some cultures shun a more 'effeminate' boy or a 'tom boyish' girl, labeling them as outside the norm and often ostracising them. This creates undo confusion in those young minds, causing them in some cases to question their gender preferences. Once the labels of 'gay' or 'lesbian' are put out there as explanations, it is an easy step for them to mistakenly believe this as the *reason* for these same gender feelings. In extreme cases, some are drawn to even doubt their gender altogether. But it is clear that if you are born with a stick you are meant to be a male, or with a hole, a female.

As I said, I am highly sympathetic to those who have deep genuine feelings for a same gender person. But when that relationship turns sexual in nature, then beauty turns to depravity, and purity becomes impurity. Another crude way of putting it is that a stick is designed for a hole and a hole to receive a stick, not a stick with a stick or a hole with a hole.

This all applies to heterosexuality alike. When sexual intimacy is engaged in outside of marriage, a loss of part of your soul occurs.

Thank God for sparing me this error through my years of ignorance and unbelief!

I realize this can be a very culturally touchy subject, but the purpose of this book is to encourage a lifestyle that follows a biblical culture, not a man-made outlook.

Loving others of both genders is God-given. When a biblical culture admonishes us to 'love one another as He has loved us' (John 13:34), it does not distinguish the gender of the receiving party. God loves everyone completely no matter which gender they are. It does mandate that this love for others be in the same manner in which He loves us. Yes, intimately and deeply, but not sexually, a gift reserved for one and one alone in the bonds of marriage.

I know many of my same gender preference friends would love to get married to each other, but we all have our own crosses to bear in this world for His Kingdom. My take on this would be to suggest that a man who is attracted to another of the same gender, be given the freedom to deeply care and interrelate with that person, but still marry from among the opposite sex, for God's intention of a 'helper suitable'; similarly so, for a woman.

This allows sexual union to play its role for procreation, and offers the person the right to purely love whomever God puts in their path for ministry.

There have been certain men I have deeply cared about over the years, some with great companionship and camaraderie, but the sexual part of my life is, and always will be reserved for my wife alone. There is no other path for those who would live a biblical culture, as servants of the King.

MARRIAGE

*If you get out there and
serve the Lord with all you have,
you can be assured He will
bring someone alongside you
or you alongside them,
designed by Him to
wonderfully enhance your
mission in His service.*

Now, who would have thought a section of thoughts on marriage would commence with, 'Don't'? But that is precisely what God, through Paul recommends.

"I want you to be free from concern. One who is unmarried is concerned about the things of the Lord, how he may please the Lord; but the one who is married is concerned about the things of the world, how he may please his wife, and his interests are divided." 1 Corinthians 7:32-34a

The passage goes on to recommend the same for women. His point was *"to secure* undistracted devotion to the Lord" (verse35b).

This is the ideal scenario for one living a biblical culture, and yet for most of us this is not tenable. He further explains,

"But I say to the unmarried and to widows that it is good to remain even as I. But if they do not have self-control, let them marry; for it is better to marry than to burn." Verses 8-9

So for the majority of us, our passions move us to marriage. Marriage is a great thing. It was instituted by God, and pictured back in the Garden of Eden, even before the fall of man. "For this cause a man shall leave his father and his mother, and shall cleave to his wife; and they shall become one flesh" (Genesis 2:24).

Marriage is so sacred, God likened it to the relationship between Christ and His Church. Ephesians 5:22-25 cites,

"Wives, be subject to your own husbands, as to the Lord. For the husband is the head of the wife, as Christ also is the head of the church, He Himself being the Savior of the body. But as the church is subject to Christ, so also the wives ought to be to their husbands in everything. Husbands, love your wives, just as Christ also loved the church and gave Himself up for her;"

The marriage relationship flourishes to the degree it models the relationship Christ displays with His church.

The passage concludes with, "let each individual among you also love his own wife even as himself; and *let* the wife *see to it* that she respect her husband" (verse 33). I believe God singled out these two features, *love* (from the husband) and *respect* (from the wife), because they are the most difficult for each spouse to adequately provide.

For the husband, demonstrating *tender love* and engaging in deep loving communication is ever awkward for most. We would rather 'fix the washing machine' to show our love. But your wife needs regular reassurance that your love and affection is solely directed to her and none other.

For the wife, knowing all his flaws, secret insecurities and sinful, sometimes childish behaviours, she still must rise to the challenge of offering him *respect*. By respecting him for the responsibility he bears under Christ for his family, you will instil confidence in him to succeed, rather than condemning his every mistake.

So how do we find that perfect mate in the first place? Let me first say that 'trust' in God is the best fortress in which to protect yourself. If you get out there and serve the Lord with all you have, you can be assured He will bring someone alongside you or you alongside them, designed by Him to wonderfully enhance your mission in His service.

God created Eve as a 'helper suitable' for Adam. I believe for men, *companionship* is the prime concern when considering a wife. Many focus on 'how cute she is' to their detriment. Beauty actually plays a much less significant role in a marriage than one would imagine, compared to trust, loyalty, security and love.

Setting aside the attraction of her outer beauty, the godly character of her nature should be paramount. Proverbs 31:10-31 wondrously details a list of qualities, none of which describe her outward attractiveness. In fact, verse 30 declares, "Charm is deceitful and beauty is vain, *but* a woman who fears the Lord, she shall be praised."

Beyond finding a 'helper', lays the challenge of uncovering someone 'suitable'. It is commonly said that 'opposites attract' and I believe this is actually by God's design. Debi and I are quite opposite. Many of her gifts are my weaknesses and my strengths her weaker points. We have learned over the years not to be threatened or annoyed by each other's differences, rather we benefit greatly from them. We are at our best, and much more effective in ministry, when I draw on her strengths and she on mine. We really do *complete* each other in so many ways.

In terms of a lasting marriage, my simple advice is to figure it out as you go, but make sure you work at it together as a team, with much prayer and discussion. Never even consider divorce, for there is nothing that cannot be overcome if you are both willing. If one party is unwilling, or abusive, then 'separation' is sometimes necessary (see

1 Corinthians 7:10-11), but always with a view to reconciliation. God gives us the "ministry of reconciliation" (2 Corinthians 5:18b), through the power of His Spirit within us, to confess our sins, repent and turn from them, and be reconciled with God.

In answer to the question of divorce, Jesus responded:

"Have you not read that He who created them from the beginning MADE THEM MALE AND FEMALE, and said "FOR THIS CAUSE A MAN SHALL LEAVE HIS FATHER AND MOTHER, AND SHALL CLEAVE TO HIS WIFE, AND THE TWO [no place for multiple husbands or wives here] SHALL BECOME ONE FLESH? "Consequently they are no longer two, but one flesh. What therefore God has joined together, let no man separate."
Matthew 19:4-6

Once you become 'one flesh', you are not to be joined to another unless one of you dies, then you are free from the union (see Romans 7:1-3). As I mentioned though, in cases of abusive or unmanageable situations it may become necessary to separate, but always with a view toward reconciliation (see 1 Corinthians 7:10-11). The exception clause for divorce is found in Matthew 5:32, "for *the* cause of unchastity". God hates divorce, and this is a last resort; when one spouse chooses to leave, and becomes 'one flesh' with another, thus breaking the spiritual symbol of faithful union between Christ and His Bride, the Church.

One of the best ways to head off divorce is by how you start a marriage in the first place. It is not meant to be a *contractual* relationship; it is designed by God for a man and a woman to become so enraptured and intertwined with each other, especially spiritually, that they will never come undone. In Deuteronomy 24:5, one of the regulations proclaimed by God was:

"When a man takes a new wife, he shall not go out with the army, nor be charged with any duty; he shall be free at home one year and shall give happiness to his wife whom he has taken."

Now I know for many cultures today, built on the monetary system, this is not tenable. But the principle remains, that we are to focus intently on building a strong new marriage relationship, and forego other commitments for the first season of life together!

I could not be happier with my own journey into marriage. Debi had been a Christian for only three months, off the streets of Vancouver, and I had just graduated Bible College in Toronto, two weeks prior to our first meeting in the foyer of Banff Park Church. Both of us had just separately come before God, proclaiming we were satisfied in Him and not looking for a mate. Our life together began in a spiritual mentoring/studying relationship with God, and blossomed over time. We soon gained the assurance He had led us to each other for more than just personal ministry. He was melding us together to serve Him as leaders in His church, and around the world!

Our wedding day was full of love and purity, with few regrets leading up to it, and has since been a path neither of us would trade for anything. Today we continue together in His service as disciples, knit closely together by the Lord, still trying to daily live a biblical culture for the benefit of all the precious souls around us! Glory to His Name!

FAMILY

Every child is different,
and needs to be treated uniquely.

Debi and I have been gifted by God with three amazing grown children. David, like his mother, is an artistic sort, blending his emotional and practical sides in a sometimes tumultuous journey with God. Emily, like her Daddy, is rather quiet and independent, but laughs from deep down and provides great strength and loyalty to those around her. Matthew, who takes after both of us, wakes up slowly, then grabs each day for all it's worth and influences everyone he bumps into along the way.

Have you ever heard someone declare, "She's just like her father!", or "He's as stubborn as his mother!" Well I believe there is an actual reason behind this! I have a theory about birth order. It stems from years of personal observation and spiritual counselling. Here it is...

As children are birthed from a couple, the firstborn tends to become more like the parent of the opposite sex. For example, if the firstborn of a couple is male, then he receives more of the traits of his mother, taking on many of her characteristics and looks. The second born takes on more of the characteristics of the other parent from the firstborn, whether a male or female. The third born receives an even mix of both parents. Then the cycle repeats itself with further offspring (Of course, this theory breaks down if there are abortions or multiple fathers/mothers involved).

BIRTH ORDER THEORY CHART

Parents
(One Marriage)

FIRSTBORN

Boy	Girl
(Most like Mother)	(Most like Father)

SECOND BORN
(Most like opposite parent of firstborn)

THIRD BORN
(Equal mix of both parents)

FOURTH
(Above pattern repeats)

I believe this is God's unique and amazing way to maintain balance and creativity throughout the generations, by mixing the DNA of the parents in this way. Imagine if every child was born very analytical, or completely creative... both would lead to very different and chaotic worlds. Without this provision everyone could potentially become 'left brained' or 'right brained', and some of the needed gifts in the world would become extinct. This marvellous provision retains the needed diversity of all types of individuals in the most natural way possible, by the Great Orchestrator of all things! While this is not found in Scripture, in my observation it has displayed a high degree of accuracy.

Now a parent may recoil, "That's wrong. My firstborn is NOTHING like me!" But close observation will reveal the opposite. Many people, who have experienced varying damage or abuse in life, will see themselves differently, or try to act other than they really are inside, thus appearing on the surface to negate this theory.

So how does all of this really matter anyway? I have found this information useful in two very prominent ways. First, it has helped me as I have counselled families over the years. In counselling it is important to gain an understanding of the person seeking your guidance to navigate difficult life issues. Knowing the parents of the client gives clues as to the origins of their issue(s). With this theory, knowing the *birth order* further aids the comprehension. If the client takes after the mother, then knowing how the mother deals with life provides an even more precise understanding of the processes used by the client, for example.

Second, it offers greater understanding of how to raise your own children. Anyone who has raised kids comes to realize that every child is different and needs to be treated uniquely. One child may be quite compliant, while another more rebellious. Using birth order tendencies provides a greater understanding of each child's needs.

Knowing how they are similar to yourself or your spouse are great clues as to how to treat them, how to discipline them most effectively, and what their prominent needs might be. Often the parent most like the child will have greater difficulty dealing with them. The traits you dislike in yourself will be the very things that bother you about that similar child. Knowing this theory can actually help you as parents to decide which one is best suited to deal with a particular child in a certain situation.

For example, when our David was young, he would respond much better to me than to Debi. The very things that drew me to fall in love with my wife were similar things that drew me to David, leading me to have great compassion for his kind of problems.

Now each individual is uniquely designed by God, but these tendencies can really help you have greater understanding of your friends and neighbours too, as you come to know their family histories. This will, in turn, give you greater empathy and impact for their needs as well.

YOUTH

*I believe the rules and regulations
should be enforced most strictly
at a very young age, and then
gradually reduced as the child grows
into a teen and toward adulthood,
not the other way around.*

"When I was a child I used to speak as a child, think as a child, reason as a child; when I became a man, I did away with childish things" (1 Corinthians 13:11). All of us, who live to adulthood, pass through this amazingly crazy period of *adolescence*! Some, however, reach the age of forty, fifty, even sixty and have not given up some of those 'childish things'. These are the things foolishly done through lack of foresight, lack of instruction or just through downright disobedience. What is a parent to do?

Scripture exhorts us to, "Train up a child in the way he should go, even when he is old he will not depart from it" (Proverbs 22:6). Note it does not say in the way you 'prefer' him to go. It does not say 'in the way you went', nor 'in the way that will make him rich'. It clearly states the way he 'should' go. What is this 'way'? Well, the Bible advises, "Remember also your Creator in the days of your youth" (Ecclesiastes 12:1a). In Jesus' day, biblical instruction was given priority throughout the years of childhood, right up to age twelve, above any other body of knowledge. It laid the foundation for viewing all else in the world, and the surrounding culture in particular.

I have always loved being around teenagers. Some dread this passage of time, but it continues to be an invigorating delight for me. You see, a young child tends to believe whatever they are taught by their parents. As they interact more and more with peers, however, they are presented with alternate viewpoints, lifestyles and sometimes polar opposite ideas from those they have been given in the home. But around the commencement of teenage years it is like life begins all over again. The young person moves from 'Here is what my parents believe' toward 'Here is what I believe'. This change can be very threatening to parents, or it can be a beautiful transition from parent to peer in the family relationship. Some parents give little thought or instruction to children, and then when they begin to 'rebel' (i.e. establish independent thoughts and values), the parents enforce stricter rules and regulations. Normally this backfires. As the teen continues the quest for independent truth and survival amongst his peers, he will hide his behaviour from his parents, and enter a dangerously secretive life, without the proper guidance needed to navigate the choices made.

I believe the rules and regulations should be enforced most strictly from a very young age (and by parental example... not, 'do as I say, not as I do') and then gradually reduced as the child grows into a teen and toward adulthood. Even if this means that foolish choices are embarked upon, at least they can continue to be discussed and guided.

The Bible verse mentioned at the outset indicates that children will and do act foolishly. It is part of the learning curve of life. Our job is not to prevent all acts of foolishness, but to instruct children in how to uncover God's ways for themselves (hopefully not just our brand of religion). This IS the 'way they should go'; to learn how to study and uncover the truth of God's Word, and respond properly to it.

Too often parents tell their kids what and how to believe, and force them to sit quietly in a church pew listening to years of sermons, whose contents are largely the RESULT of another's study and not the 'path' for uncovering God's Word for themselves. Small wonder so many children rebel from attending church in the teen years.

If we are to maintain close relations with our growing youth, we must have taught them how to learn from God and His Word, how to accept Christ for themselves and how to be guided by the Spirit of God. Then, as they emerge from childhood, through some 'foolishness', it will be vital to transition gradually from parent to peer, from autocracy to democracy; to engage in conversation and begin learning from them. Ask their advice on some matters. In essence, move toward treating them as responsible adults, rather than foolish children. This is a difficult manoeuvre, which is why it is dreaded by so many who simply feel ill-equipped for the task.

Let me give it to you from the teen point of view. You have always believed whatever your parents have told you. They have always been your security and the compass for your life. But as your hormones come alive, all of a sudden what your peers say and do, and especially how they think of you begins to overshadow the priorities of home life. At this juncture a marvellous, yet terrifying thing occurs. You must start life all over again. There is a great insecurity that arises within, but a greater need to 'look cool' and in charge on the outside.

So begins the source of the grand transition. The youth needs to develop his own set of beliefs, based now upon the entire world around him and not just from the home. The navigational dangers are all the new influences upon his belief system. He is expected by whoever become the most influential peers, to adopt their beliefs and behaviours, many of which may be contrary to his own.

So if you as parents at this point are to retain your influence, you must begin to reduce the rules and regulations, not increase them. You must allow for some foolishness, applaud the victories, trust in what has been planted from God in the days of their youth, and in God to carry them onward to the point of agedness. Stricter rules most often create hidden behaviour and eliminate the valuable conversations that could be engaged in at those opportune moments.

This is one of the reasons I have loved being around teenagers. Because they have to appear 'cool', while internally figuring life out all over again for themselves, they will look for non-threatening adults to help them sort it all out. Where parents cannot fill some of this role, Youth Pastors, Senior Pastors and other adults who are willing to take a direct interest in a few teens can make some of the greatest contributions to their young lives. As a parent, welcome those responsible adults who engage in conversation with your teen. They may produce more fruit than you at this point.

Know this though... mistakes WILL be made... and not all of them will be made by the teen! Be quick to say sorry, and don't neglect outlining your own faults in the sometimes tense moments that will inevitably come as they journey toward 'putting away foolish things'.

AMBITION

*Personal ambition takes you
from the 'pack of your peers',
to the purpose for which he
placed you among them.*

*It moves you from
being 'influenced',
to being influential.*

Let me express to the youth: as you move toward adulthood, it will become important for you to begin exploring why God made you, and what He designed you to be doing in His world. What is it that drives you? What has He placed on your heart that motivates you with passion? What ambitions has He uniquely designed you to pursue? For without ambition you will not properly 'fit' within a society.

Without ambition you begin to suffer from lethargy, which makes you susceptible to adverse peer pressure from within your surrounding culture. Many young people especially fall into a great bondage of wanting nothing more than to be 'acceptable' to those around them. As a result, they are often influenced into immoral, even illegal behaviour in an attempt to 'fit in'. Ambition counteracts this vulnerability. Personal ambition takes you from the 'pack' of your peers, to the 'purpose' for which He placed you among them. It moves you from being the 'influenced,' to being influential.

In 2 Corinthians 5:9 Paul purports, "Therefore also we have as our ambition, whether at home or absent, to be pleasing to Him." Ambition is meant to be inspired by God-given gifts, personality and aptitudes. Whether becoming a painter, philosopher, musician or welder, ambitions lend themselves to creating a 'fit' within the surrounding culture. They make you a productive member of your community and a contributor to its health.

Personality contributes to placement in a culture as well. Let me explain. If a person is a happy, bubbly individual, then he or she 'fits in' wherever there is a need or desire for that type of person; at a backyard BBQ, in a sales office, etc. Someone who loves to paint portraits 'fits in' well on the streets of Paris, teaching in an arts school or drawing caricatures at a fall fair.

I have counselled many individuals whose significant root problem stems from either depressingly futile or destructively successful attempts to be acceptable and 'liked' by their peers, to the exclusion of their own personal ambitions.

Here is where the Triune God again brings healing and health. By discovering the will of God unique to your life and living, incorporating the mind of Christ to sort out the pathway, and drawing on the Holy Spirit of God for confidence and strength to pursue your ambition, the 'fit' takes care of itself. You will emerge into the culture as a useful, sought after individual for the very qualities and skills you possess.

God took me down the path of a quiet and thoughtful disciple-maker. I became utilized by those around me for spiritual direction and instruction. That has been a 'fit' for me occupationally and personally throughout my life. My personality leads me to personal and thoughtful conversations with individuals, even in a noisy large group setting. This means that I do not 'fit' as the 'life of the party' at a raucous get together, nor do I turn heads when I enter a room. But I am satisfied with the roles God has given me to contribute in His world, so the rest has no bearing on my self-worth or level of contentment.

If we can uncover and release the inner ambitions God has particularly and wonderfully designed us for, we will always 'fit' in the very places and positions we are needed most by whatever culture He places us in. Our ambition, especially as a profession, should bring us great purpose and satisfaction wherever we venture... and generally makes us effective for others!

96

PLANNING

I have found it imperative to
read His Word (hear from Him)
and pray (respond to Him),
before I do anything else
in the morning.

So what role does God play in the developing of your ambitions? Who decides what you will do with your life? I would suggest you are meant to work in tandem with Him, as His thoughtful and passionate servant.

"The mind of man plans his way, but the Lord directs his steps" (Proverbs 16:9). If the Lord takes an active, personal role in directing my steps, then He must 'have' a path for me to follow. But I suspect this path is not solely about me and my plans, like what job I will have, or which marriage partner I get. I sense it is more about how He designed me in my DNA.

He teaches us to deny ourselves and follow Him. Denying self logically leads to considering others. To consider another means to serve in some way. So part of the direction I receive from Him involves influencing others in practical, and ultimately spiritual ways. The way He made me will direct what kind of service I render to the community around me. Depending on my design, I may make my plan to participate in the arts (music, painting, photography, dance, etc.) or in business (owner, employee, entrepreneur, etc.) or a host of other possibilities. I will offer some sort of service or product to contribute to the wellbeing of those around me.

So as I plan and begin to make goals in a specific direction, given my unique makeup, He begins to direct me to the people He wants me to contribute to, according to my God-given giftings.

I believe there must be a balance between order and spontaneity here, a wonderful cooperation between our mind and the mind of Christ. Jesus called for order both in the church gathered and in the daily lives of each member. In the church gathered we are advised, "But let all things be done properly and in an orderly manner" (1 Corinthians 14:40), and yet we must leave room for the leading of the Spirit. This integration of human and Divine extends into our daily lives as well. I believe He gave us the capacity under His guidance to plan out our day, but I equally believe we must leave room for redirection and unanticipated needs around us. Over time it becomes an intimate relationship of daily planning and being daily directed through the journey of this one life experience on earth.

For example, in Acts 8 Philip made a plan. He went down to Samaria to 'proclaim Christ' to them (verse 5). After a season of ministry, he started back to Jerusalem (verse 25). But then "an angel of the Lord spoke to Philip saying, "Arise and go south"... And he arose and went" (verses 26-27). Here we have a beautiful picture of this balance between the organized plans of your life and the spontaneous leading of the Spirit within that framework, between the plans of man and the overriding directives of God.

Let me share how this has played out in my own life. As the larger journey of my life plans unfolded, there came significant points where God prompted me to follow certain directives. For me, if I sensed something in my mind as coming from Him, rather than my own human desires, I would ask Him to remove it if it wasn't from Him. I would also ask that if it was of Him, to give me a 'lasting peace' about it within my soul. This lasting peace would then give me the confidence to proceed and act upon His directive, even if it seemed 'crazy' or 'far-fetched' to others. His pleasure must trump well-meaning observers (like Job's friends).

On a more day to day basis, I have found it imperative to read His Word (hear from Him) and pray (respond to Him), before I do anything else in the morning. My heart goes out to those who are not 'morning people', but there is no logic in proceeding through your day on your own, and then hearing from Him after it is all over! No matter what time constraint is placed upon you to arrive at your workplace, just get up early enough to allow Him first place!

In my 40 plus years of following Christ, there have only been a handful of occasions His Word has not started my day. And believe it or not, I have never had a cup of coffee in my whole life! HE gets me going. HE speaks to my heart and convicts me of my sin. HE enlivens me to face a dark world, and I love Him deeply for it! And if you look carefully, even Jesus made it His discipline to get off alone with the Father 'prior' to spiritual ministry, thus ensuring He was obeying what the Father initiated for Him to do.

So to continue, once my day commences, I carry on a running conversation with my Lord. This 'praying without ceasing' (1 Thessalonians 5:17) gives me the greatest chance to do things His way, approach people with His heart and engage the culture with His wisdom, maintaining an eternal perspective of His greater purposes over my unfolding day.

Living a biblical culture is not disassociating yourself from the culture you live in, rather it is engaging the culture with the "fruit of the Spirit" (Galatians 5:22-23) in all 'purity' (verse 24) and 'humility' (verse 26). So if I am at the office and heading toward a meeting, how God leads me to interact with people along that hallway could make a spiritual difference to their lives. I often plan a little extra time around me to ensure I can 'linger' for a helpful conversation, rather than speed by everyone to stay on task, should God so lead. This better ensures I have some 'God stories' to share by the end of every week!

I implore you to do something similar; to have a strategy for being intertwined with Him in such a way as to respond to His leading you outside the plans of your day.

WORK

Work, that you might have to share,
not have to acquire and possess.

Concerning work, let me say this right up front... in order to live out a biblical culture you do not have to take on a 'religious' oriented occupation. Jesus never forbade nor mandated any type of useful and gainful employment. But where did work come from? Well, ever since Adam and Eve disobeyed in the garden, men have been required to 'toil' for sustenance (Genesis 3:17). Women were given a different punishment, but men were tasked with working 'by the sweat of their brows'. Proverbs 31:10-31 lists a number of areas an 'excellent wife' puts her hands to as well, but these are out of love for her family and the needy around her, not a necessary consequence of sin.

There is an awesome little verse found in Ephesians 4:28 which aptly defines a biblical purpose for *work*. It simply states,

"Let him who steals steal no longer; but rather let him labor [work], performing with his own hands what is good, in order that he may have something to share with him who has need."

Wow! What a completely contrary view from the frightfully commonplace, 'I'm gonna buy myself a new...'. Imagine *working* to share with one who has need! What a heavenly picture of purpose and meaning! Working is biblically intended as a means to provide for others; my wife, my family, my needy neighbours and the unfairly impoverished around the world. It sounds to me very much like the second greatest commandment given by Jesus: "You shall LOVE YOUR NEIGHBOUR AS YOURSELF" (Mark 12:31).

Work is not primarily a means to acquire and possess, rather a means to share, to give, to fill the gaps of genuine need. And notice the phrase 'performing with his own hands what is good'. To me, this speaks of at least two important related issues. First, it speaks to the godly character required for the labour. We are called to work at things that are 'good', not shady, nor illegal, not with income inequality, not with unfair profit margins nor deceptive marketing strategies, etc. Find a suitable profession you can be spiritually proud of that benefits society, and then enjoy sharing the income procured from it!

Second, 'performing with your own hands' speaks against the abuse of 'hand-outs' whether from governments, family or friends. Help is meant to be temporary, in times of 'distress' (see James 1:27). For example, living off government aid as a lifestyle instead of con-tinually pursuing employment makes you a drain on the hard work of others, rather than being a productive part of society. This 'love of the money of others' engenders all sorts of destructive tendencies and contributes to the degrading of the culture you live in.

CAREER

By around 30 years of age
each person should have found
their 'fit' in society,
and for the next twenty years
become a positive force
in the workplace.

One of the patterns I have chosen as a rough personal career guide throughout my life journey is based upon how God set things up for the Levitical Temple service in the Old Testament.

LIFE/CAREER CHART

A biblical model from God's Levitical Temple Service

AGE	DESCRIPTION	SAMPLE SOURCE
1 month – 12	Taught Bible and biblical lifestyle	"Adult Age," McClintock and Strong's Encyclopaedia
12 – 14	Girls could marry @ 12, boys @ 14, with parental consent	
12 – 20	General public education	
20 – 25	Assist with the service of the house of the Lord	2 Chronicles 31:17
25 – 30	Enter to perform service in the work of the tent of meeting	Numbers 8:24
30 – 50	Enter house of the Lord for his daily obligations/oversee the work	Numbers 4:3 2 Chronicles 31:16
50+	Retire from service in the work May assist, but no work themselves	Numbers 8:25 Numbers 8:26

If you search carefully through the Old Testament books of Numbers and Chronicles, you will discover actual ages delineated for certain types of service within the temple operation. The *chart* above outlines these stages.

Biblical historians, studying Judaism of the time, indicate that the children received Bible education almost exclusively up to the age of twelve. Further, boys could marry or make religious vows as early as 14 years old and girls at 12 years old, both only with parental permission. Their *public* education commenced from twelve years old through to the age of twenty.

Here is where it gets interesting. From twenty to twenty five years of age the Levitical students became responsible to 'assist with the service' (2 Chronicles 31:17), and had general *duties*. In effect, they carried things around for the priests, observing how everything worked in the temple. From age twenty five to thirty they 'performed service' (Numbers 8:24). It was during the last half of their twenty's that they apprenticed for a specific aspect of service in the tent of meeting. Then from thirty to fifty they had their 'daily obligations' (2 Chronicles 31:16). This was the twenty year period spanning their *career* in temple service. At the age of fifty, they were required to 'cease work' (Numbers 8:25) in the temple. They were permitted to 'assist others' (Numbers 8:26) after that, but could have no more personal responsibilities.

Here are some of the practical things I have found helpful to extrapolate from this pattern.

First of all, how wonderful that the Bible was so readily used for early instruction. Children are born prepared to learn. Educators tell us children cultivate 85 percent of their intellect, personality and skills by the age of five.[1] I find that pretty staggering. How well advised we are to ensure the Bible is a major portion of the earliest instruction. Sadly, many expend much more energy getting kids into 'sports' than Bible reading. I propose that proper understanding of the Bible will better instruct our children in the values of team building, cooperating with others, healthy self-image, activity, etc. than sports teams claim to provide; and so much more. Now I am certainly not slamming sports, but even the Word proclaims,

"bodily discipline is only of little profit, but godliness is profitable for all things, since it holds promise for the present life and also for the life to come." 1 Timothy 4:8

Now, I am certain to offend some sports proponents here, but please ask yourself how much of your decision to place your kids in sports and the like is due to 'cultural' pressure, and how much for 'biblical' reasons? It is for you to decide.

Second, is the issue of delaying the age of marriage, probably the greatest factor relating to sexual promiscuity among teenagers and twenty something's. Under Judaism, boys could marry or make religious vows at 14-years-old and girls at 12-years-old, both only with parental permission, which parental permission was required until both boys and girls were 21-years-old.[2] As I mentioned earlier on, how unfortunate so many of our cultures promote delaying marriage years beyond puberty, for the excuses of education, money and maturity. I believe we were meant to 'have' a spouse not too long after the age God built it into us to HAVE the urge.

In North American culture, for example, many tell our children to 'abstain', to 'take a cold shower', to 'get involved in hobbies', 'to be home before dark', anything to keep their minds off sex. My view is that marriages should be fostered at much earlier ages, and young married teens continue to be cared for by supportive parents through the initial years of that marriage.

Third, I believe cultures that overemphasize specialized higher education are creating artificial and inappropriate stresses upon new young generations of people. We start demanding our kids 'decide' what they are going to do in life far too early. We do it because they are finishing high school at seventeen or eighteen and 'need' to pick a career to pursue in University or college. I have found it more helpful to follow the priestly temple oriented pattern when counselling youth. By 'twenty' they should be starting to toss around some career ideas, getting some experience, even volunteering in a variety of fields, to help narrow down what gives them passion and creates ambition within them. I suggest they try out some different jobs, job shadow various career professionals, seeking the path forward. At 'twenty five' our children do not yet need to be successful professionals, but beginning apprentices, within the narrowed down fields of interest.

By around thirty years of age each person should have found their 'fit' in society and for the next twenty years become a positive force in the workplace, for the benefit of the cultural society they live in.

Lastly, at around fifty years of age there should be a 'season of life' shift toward passing on your valuable experience and knowledge to those young up and coming assistants and apprentices who will then take over and powerfully contribute to the generation of your own children. Holding on to your 'spot' until our artificially manufactured retirement age of 65 or beyond, denies the younger ones the opportunity to take your place, and risks your own contributions becoming increasingly irrelevant.

For example, one of the troubling things I have observed among the beloved church families is the decline of some, almost to extinction. The cause for this sharp decline is often due to leadership above the age of fifty, fearing the 'younger' leaders will somehow change and thus destroy everything. Our businesses and churches would be well served to build 'mentoring/transitioning' functions into their very fabric. While continuing to provide for the valued older employees, they can start replacing their functioning with younger ones, full of new fresh passion and entrepreneurial spirit.

MONEY

Money is meant to be a tool,
not a desire.

This leads us into the next topic of consideration, *money*. In our day and age, most cultures have moved from self- sustaining farming or trading economies to a monetary system. Since most of us now need 'money' as a means to provide, we must all find a way to bring in a steady supply of it. So how do 'money' and 'work' align with living out a biblical culture?

First, the Bible speaks clearly against the *love* of money. Ecclesiastes 5:10 reads, "He who loves money will not be satisfied with money nor he who loves abundance *with* its income." In Luke 16:14 the Pharisees were scolded by Jesus for being "lovers of money". 1 Timothy 3:3 warns us to be "free from the love of money", and Hebrews 13:5 exhorts us to "Let your character be free from the love of money."

Why is the love of money so dangerous? Well, the oft quoted 1 Timothy 6:10 explains,

"For the love of money is a root of all sorts of evil, and some by longing for it have wandered away from the faith, and pierced themselves with many a pang."

The biblical corollary to this is found in the very next verse,

"But flee from these things, you man of God; and pursue righteousness, godliness, faith, love, perseverance and

gentleness. Fight the good fight of faith; take hold of the eternal
life to which you were called!"   *1 Timothy 6:11*

I believe we are exhorted here to keep our focus off the money being acquired and concentrate instead on building the godly character that will shape the best use of the money we are given from our work, maintaining the values of an eternal perspective.

Money is meant simply to be a tool, not a desire. The focus is not to be getting as much as possible, but having the exact amount to participate in whatever activities God leads you into. The problem is not the money itself, but the lure of what money can get you. It is the link to greed and the desire for possessions and pleasures that make it so insidious.

For those wanting to live a biblical culture, money should be viewed as providing the means for truly helping others. It is vital to maintain a heavenly perspective on what we ourselves actually 'need' in our own life, learning to be content with whatever He provides.

NEEDS

I now see everything other than
water, health-giving food,
clothing, and basic shelter
as a BONUS, not a requirement
for my contentment.

There is nothing wrong
with possessions or wealth,
but they must be held lightly.

Now what causes a 'love of money' in the first place? Is it not discontentment? Most cultures are economically driven and propelled by the desire for more than we have. Media and retail establishments often feed our discontentment by deceiving us into purchasing the latest and greatest everything! So what do we actually NEED in our lives? Again, the Bible offers up a marvellously simple and insightful verse tucked away in 1 Timothy 6:8. It simply says,

"If we have food and covering, with these we shall be content."

This one verse has helped revolutionize how I view possessions... this by itself is worth the price of the book! I now see everything other than water, health-giving food, clothing and basic shelter as a BONUS, not a requirement for my contentment as I journey through this world. I no longer complain about wanting more, or what I 'need' to make me happy. And my life has been so much richer for it.

The following verse expands on this thought;

"But those who want to get rich fall into temptation and a snare and many foolish and harmful desires which plunge men into ruin and destruction."

What a poignant visual illustration is the 'snare'. Desirous food is tangled in plain sight on the regular path of an animal, but beneath it lays a set of jaws to fully capture the creature that goes after the food. How similar are the myriad of accessory stores dangled before us on a daily basis, to tempt us with purchases that will ultimately capture our hearts and further distract us from the service of our King!

A biblical culture accepts this scriptural admonition not to be ensnared by discontentment and longing after more and more. Friends, possessions, comforts, accessories, transportation means and the like are all added blessings. They should be received with thanksgiving to whatever degree they are provided, and utilized in His service.

Now poverty and wealth both have their inherent dangers. Agur, the writer of Proverbs 30 insightfully requested:

"Two things I have asked of Thee, do not refuse me before I die: Keep deception and lies far from me, give me neither poverty nor riches; feed me with the food that is my portion, lest I be full and deny Thee and say, "Who is the Lord?" or lest I be in want and steal, and profane the name of my God."   Proverbs 30:7-9

The secret in both instances is 'contentment', so neither the temptations of stealing or neglecting become a reality.

There is nothing wrong with possessions, or wealth, but they must be held 'lightly'. Remember when Jesus told his disciples to go into town and fetch a donkey and a colt? (Matthew 21:2-7) If the owner had not possessed a colt, Jesus would not have been able to use it for God's glory to enter Jerusalem on His way to the cross. And consider carefully the words He told His disciples to say to the owner: "The Lord has need of them" (verse 3). This is the posture we should have with all our possessions and wealth. When the Master 'has need of them' they are given, without hesitation and with great joy. What a privilege to have all my possessions ready and at His service!

What a tragedy that so commonplace in most of our human cultures are the many complaints; the traffic jam, the long checkout line at the store, how someone kept us waiting ten whole minutes, how terrible our dad is because he won't buy me the newest phone on the market... so many seemingly justifiable annoyances in life. I am so grateful that God has given my wife and I the opportunity to serve amongst the most needy in various places around the globe, to gain a great appreciation for every little added blessing... INCLUDING enough food and covering!

FOOD

Eat for health,
not for taste!

Forgive me if I add a word about food. One of the more neglected propensities, in some cases addictions in most of the wealthier cultures is the improper intake of food. Here is an idiom I have found SO helpful, that serves a biblical culture: 'Eat for health, not for taste!' As a culture develops greater financial resources, the food industry often becomes one of the most invasive sources of temptation. Now God certainly gave us the taste buds to enjoy the sensation of what our mouth consumes, but becoming enslaved to taste was never His intention.

God "supplies us with all things to enjoy" (1 Timothy 6:17b), but NOT to be ruled by. And 'all things' certainly does not extend to improper or impure things. So give your body what it needs to function efficiently and properly, in the greater pursuit of a biblical culture of obedience and service to the King of kings.

Taste should not trump health in your life if you are committed to being a disciple of the Lord Jesus. How can you follow His lead to help the needy people on top of that mountain, if you can't even climb the mountain? How can you be alert each day to the assignments He puts in your path if you are weary and lethargic? And, no, you do not NEED your cup of coffee to jump start your day! You need the energy of the Holy Spirit, the fortification of the Word of God and a passion for Jesus, to properly prepare for each day. Fuelling your body properly goes a long way toward providing the human energy and persistence needed to engage with all three Persons of the Trinity.

As each new day dawns, He will reveal your next exciting purpose for being created, and give you the strength to positively influence your culture! Those who skip breakfast miss the point that a body needs fuelling prior to functioning, especially since it has had no fuel through the entire night. We should provide it with some healthy nourishment, then expend some energy, then fuel it again for more propulsion, with the smallest portions consumed at the end of the day, when little more will be expended while sleeping. For proper service to the Kingdom, remember, sugar and starch are not primary food groups! LOL

CLASSES

What we need is a 'biblical' class,
which takes the godly parts
of each economic tier
and marries them
into a lifestyle
that fits everywhere
in the world.

'Love your Neighbour'
works in every culture!

Among the many cultures of the world we find three loosely defined economic tiers, which some label 'lower', 'middle' and 'upper' class. These structures are transcultural in that they display certain commonalities around the world. As such, they become a kind of culture of their own. While most view upward mobility as the 'goal', I believe each class contains its own potential bondage that can chain people to emptiness, and often to hopelessness. We see some extremely wealthy people overdosing, many middle class expending thirty years of their lives waiting for retirement, and large numbers of poor folks giving up hope of ever feeling positive about their future. We also see shining examples of those with great freedom and joy in each of the classes.

My proposal here is that by understanding the different values, thought patterns, survival strategies and social interactions distinct to each class, you will have greater effectiveness in communicating the gospel.

I was recently handed a book from a fellow missionary entitled, "Understanding Poverty", by Ruby Payne.[3] I highly recommend it for those working cross-class in any setting. In this work, the author wonderfully uncovers the 'hidden rules' of each class, especially among the impoverished.

Here are a few samples. First, 'Money' amongst the poor is "to be spent"; for the middle class it is "to be saved"; for the wealthy it is "to be invested". I have added a fourth category: 'Biblical' class. For this group, I suggest, money is 'to be held lightly, and used wisely' (see Luke 18:22-30).

When we first moved to Honduras we thought we should raise people out of poverty. Coming from a middle class background, it seemed the right thing to do. We started giving people things, thinking it would give them the tools to prosper. What frustration followed when all we gave was immediately used up, spent, or given away. Seemingly, no matter what we did, they started every new day financially at *zero*. We tried to mobilize them to save money and accumulate for the future, but to no avail.

I have since come to better understand that trying to turn a poverty culture into a middle class culture actually does more harm than good. They have us beat on having a deep sense of community, of sharing the extra, of sacrificially going without to help a neighbour. Their goal is not monetary accumulation, but making sure everyone in their extended family *makes it* through the day. So now we engage them with the tools to make their lives just a little more comfortable, and help them develop small financial 'buffers', to ease the pressure of emergencies.

Here is a second sample, related to the first, concerning 'Time'. The 'present is most important' to the poor. 'Decisions are made for the moment, based on feelings or survival.' The 'future is most important' to the middle class. 'Decisions here are made against future ramifications.' And for the wealthy, 'traditions and history' take precedence. 'Decisions are made partially on the basis of tradition and decorum.'

Here I have added the biblical class ideal that 'eternity' is most import-ant. 'Decisions are made by God's prompting' (Luke 6:46).

Once we realized the future was less important among the poor, we were able to better comprehend how to help them move ahead in life economically without losing the positive ways they value.

There is another book out entitled, *"When Helping Hurts"*. The title itself provides ample warning to those coming from wealthier cultures to 'help those poor souls'. Imagine what passes through our minds here in Honduras, when people come just to build something or give handouts to a culture valuing relationship over structure. Many of the buildings lay dormant, and no matter how much food is handed out, shortly thereafter the hunger returns.

We have come to see that while handouts 'help' in emergency situations, they most often lead to one of two harmful results. Those who love the handouts start feeling *entitled* to them, and even come to demand more and more, considering *work* less appealing. Conversely, others lose their self-esteem through the shameful feelings of not be-ing able to provide for themselves.

I know I am just touching on this important and fascinating subject, but I at least wanted to stimulate your thinking, to take better stock of how you view the two classes of people you are NOT in. By taking the time to simply sit with them, get to know them and relate extensively with them, you will become so much more effective in sharing a bib-lical culture with them, rather than destructively harming them with your own tainted world view.

What we truly need is a 'biblical' class, which takes the godly parts of each economic outlook and marries them into a lifestyle that fits everywhere in the world; that makes our surroundings better every-where in the world; for 'Every good thing bestowed and every per-fect gift is from above, coming down from the Father of lights' (James 1:17a).

CHURCH

BELIEVERISM

In a sometimes desperate attempt
to equate church growth with 'success',
many churches settled for
making 'believers'.

"Go therefore and make [believers] disciples" (Matthew 28:19a).

For decades now there has been a disease infecting many of our churches, running rampant. It is the disease of 'believerism'. In a sometimes desperate attempt to equate church growth with success, many churches settled for making believers... just pray the prayer, say the words, and believe the Bible to be true. It was fostered by flashy evangelism programs, until it sadly became the norm. This growing lack of spiritual influence has been a contributing factor in the secularization of many nations.

As a result, many sit in congregations today proclaiming, "Amen Pastor!" In essence, what they really mean is, "I agree with what you are saying. I BELIEVE that to be true!" What they are not saying is, "I will respond and obey my Lord in the things you are relating to us from His Word, no matter what the cost in human terms!"

God led Debi and I to be down here in Roatan, ministering among the impoverished, but we had to choose to respond and come. While I miss close proximity with my children immensely, and I applaud them for continuing to share Debi and I with a world of spiritual children, living a biblical culture requires great sacrifice from the comforts we prefer.

While still pastoring in Canada, I showed a short clip from the TV series 'West Wing' one Sunday morning, to illustrate the point of doing more to help the world. The congregation missed the point of the values I was trying to portray through it, and some scolded me afterward because there was a swear word in the clip.

People miss the point of things... congregations largely miss the point of church gatherings, and fellowship, and discipleship. The church is imploding in Canada especially in these days because most who are the Church keep missing the point of what they are meeting for... to join in celebrating what God is doing through them all through the week they just came out of! Church is not about programs, positions, postures or politics; it is the 'assembling of ourselves together to consider how to stimulate one another to love and good deeds' (Hebrews 10:24). It is about helping each other become disciples out in the world, not merely believers in the pews. Whenever we stray from this noble vision, we need to get on our knees and apologize to God, then to one another, and get back onto the 'narrow path' again.

Happily though, I have recently observed a renewing passion for Jesus that gives me hope for the next (last?) generation, as this world rapidly darkens. It gives me hope that a new generation of young disciples will spring forth, shedding the 'traditions of men' and clinging to the great commandments. It is certainly needed in this ever secularizing globe of citizens, and my prayer is that this book will in some small way contribute to the development of souls into disciples of Christ. Believing is, of course VITAL, but it is only the first step toward a life of obedience to His will and His ways.

PURPOSE

The weekly gathering is meant to be 'inspirational',
Bible Study is meant to be 'informational',
and Small Groups are meant to be 'relational,
but it takes all three to be 'transformational'.

Go to church for what you can 'give',
not for what you can 'get'.

The church was initiated by Jesus Himself so it is a GOOD idea. It includes every person throughout human history whom God has redeemed back to Himself through the saving power of His Son. We are never to neglect gathering together with small companies of His Church as Christ followers, in a setting which includes elders, deacons and true worshippers. The Bible presumes a church will always function locally.

Gather

The purpose of regularly gathering as church congregations includes worship, prayer, instruction, fellowship and communion, and is meant to foster disciples who mutually care for each other in holistic ways.

Two of these precious reasons for gathering regularly are to worship, and to pray to God corporately. 1 Peter 2:9 calls us "A CHOSEN RACE, A royal PRIESTHOOD, A HOLY NATION, A PEOPLE FOR God's OWN POSSESSION." As such, we are to "proclaim the excellencies of Him who has called you out of darkness into His marvellous light" (verse 9b). As each of you gather to proclaim Him publicly through worship, you are, in essence, *"speaking to one another in psalms and hymns and spiritual songs, singing and making melody in your heart to the Lord; always giving thanks for all things in the name of our Lord Jesus Christ to God, even the Father;"*   Ephesians 5:19-20

These times of true worship and fervent prayer are like sweet incense to the Lord (see Revelation 5:8), and should never be hindered by battles over song preference, instrumentation or styles of music. Those are for leaders to determine as they discern our spiritual needs.

Another function of the gathered church is necessarily implied in our command to "make disciples of all nations... teaching them". Teaching the Word and ways of God occupies a vital part of why we need to be together regularly. Although the internet has an enormous volume of teaching, "iron sharpens iron" (Proverbs 27:17) best when accomplished face to face, as we journey through life's circumstances together. Alone, there are no elders to help discern your discoveries, or fellow disciples to discuss your ideas with or challenge them, when necessary.

A fourth purpose of the gathered church is for fellowship: a wonderful network of ministering relationships. Paul described it well in Romans 1:11-12,

"For I long to see you in order that I may impart some spiritual gift to you, that you may be established; that is, that I may be encouraged together with you while among you, each of us by the other's faith, both yours and mine."

When we sing, we are contributing; when we pray, we are contributing; when we listen intently to the message of the Word, we are contributing.

A great feature of corporate fellowship is other-focused biblical living.

"Do nothing from selfishness or empty conceit, but with humility of mind let each of you regard one another as more important than himself; do not merely look out for your own personal interests, but also for the interests of others."
Philippians 2:3-4

In fact, there are over 30 'one another' admonitions in the New Testament for us to be intimately engaged in with each other. This is the missing component for those who only attend church weekly, and forego ministering to each other outside the church building. At one of our churches we used the following catch phrases: "The weekly gathering is meant to be 'inspirational', Bible Study is meant to be 'informational', and Small Groups are meant to be 'relational', but it takes all three to be 'transformational'." If you don't rub spiritual shoulders with other disciples, you are in danger of not activating what you have internalized. "But prove yourselves doers of the word, and not merely hearers who delude themselves" (James 1:22). Romans 2:13 adds, "for not the hearers of the Law are just before God, but the doers of the Law will be justified."

Finally, communion, sometimes called 'The Lord's Supper', is integral. This gives worshippers the reverent opportunity to move into the holy of holies together before God, so to speak, to remember Christ's completed work. Here we humbly confess our sins and recall what precious salvation He accomplished for us on the cross, overcoming sin and death by His atoning bodily sacrifice and His shed blood. What a sobering, yet unifying time for His gathered people, to ensure we never take lightly or become forgetful of the 'Cornerstone' of our faith.

Now I have not mentioned Baptism here, for it is inherent in the teaching of the Word. Baptism is an outward symbol of the inward commitment of repentance and faith, made in Christ. Being completely immersed down into the water and then up again, offers the perfect portrayal of dying to self, sin and the stranglehold of death, and then springing forth to new life in Christ for all eternity. What a joy for the church to gather in this way to celebrate a new believer's bold public confession of their commitment to live as a disciple of Christ!

These are the core purposes for each local church. They are not man-made traditions, but precepts of God. They are not intended as 'options', as from a TV remote, but commands, necessary for Jesus' church to prevail through the generations.

For those disillusioned with the 'modern church' scenario, I have often encouraged people to try going to church for what you can 'give', not what you can 'get'. It has revolutionized the experience of many in the family of God. Before you arrive, prepare your heart and mind to minister to others. As you enter, remain alert to whomever God might lead you to, for a 'one another' opportunity. His activity should occupy your time spent there. Stay attuned to what God wants to reveal to you, but also discern how others are receiving from Him, so you can properly assist them after the service. Your hands demonstrate His love and your mouth proclaims His excellencies, and those He feeds through you will not become disillusioned themselves with His gathered people!

I have loved and served local churches since my conversion at age 15, and it is rare that I am not gathered with a group of God's people numerous times on a weekly basis. Hebrews 10:24 warns us 'not to forsake our own assembling together, as is the habit of some, but encouraging one another; and all the more, as you see the day drawing near.' Those who ignore gathering are simply not adhering to His intentions for them.

For those who attend home churches, understand that elder/leaders and deacons must be operative as a minimum for the gathering to be called a 'church' fellowship. Logically, why would God Himself list specific qualities for elders and deacons if we were not meant to have them? Those denominations or groups who bypass this precept are gravely misguiding their people. Whether you call them elders or not, they must be functioning as such, for His word presumes leaders in every church, who "keep watch over your souls, as those who will give an account" (Hebrews 13:17b).

Never give up on 'church', but work to keep it conforming to its original intent.

Study

The Bible says, "Be diligent to present yourself approved to God as a workman who does not need to be ashamed, handling accurately the word of truth" (2 Timothy 2:15). I have been in many settings amongst believers, where it actually became 'awkward' to talk about the Scriptures. We are great at small talk, but without Bible comprehension from intentional study, we can end up being biblically 'shy', due to a lack of spiritual understanding. It is like when I first attended a Spanish church service in Honduras without knowing the language. I could smile, stand, and sit when everyone else did, but that was about it. The words just left me feeling like an outsider.

For proper discipleship to occur in a maturing body, study of the Word must occupy much time and effort. 2 Timothy 2:2 reads,

"And the things which you [the student] have heard from me [the teacher] in the presence of many witnesses [gathered], these entrust to faithful men [student interaction], who will be able to teach others [students] also."

Remember, studying necessarily takes you deeper than reading. It moves you from what to why. Make sure as you read His word, that you ask a lot of questions, and then leave no question unanswered. There are many great study aids out there to assist you, but do not take their answers at face value. Take the time to ponder the passage yourself, and discuss it with others in small intentional groups.

Studying His word together with others, provides a much greater opportunity for reaching an understanding of the heart of God for your life, and the world around you.

Fellowship

Since we are built for relationship, it is vital that we interrelate with one another outside the larger gathering, not just receive a weekly morning monologue from the church stage. As I said, at least 30 distinct 'one anothers' are mentioned in the New Testament as things we are to mutually provide for each other. These interrelationships are meant to be spiritual in nature, and offered in practical ways. Here is a chart to give you ideas from the New Testament for implementing God's will in living a biblical culture:

ONE ANOTHER CHART

be at peace with	bearing with
love	comfort
be devoted to	encourage
give preference to	build up
be of the same mind toward	live in peace with
let us not judge	do not speak against
accept	do not complain against
serve	confess your sins to
don't bite and devour	pray for
not challenging	fervently love
showing tolerance for	be hospitable to
be kind to	fellowship with
be subject to	do not lie to

greet ... with a holy kiss
speaking to ... in psalms, hymns & spiritual songs
stimulate ... to love and good deeds

Let me say a word about that. 'One another' implies a mutual ministry. For example, part of church life is for me to come alongside your difficulties to 'encourage you'. But of equal importance is for you to come and encourage me when I need it. As God enables you, minister the 'one anothers' to those He prompts you toward. But let me exhort you in this... do not remain silent when you are in need of them! Never allow a personal pity party to envelope you, exclaiming that 'nobody ever cares about me when I'm in need!' Instead, call someone! It is perfectly valid to request, "Hey, I could really use some encouragement right about now. Could we please get together?" We are 'members' of one another and should be available to bestow His grace upon others, but also to expect others to be available for us in times of need.

It is through the integration of closely knit lives within smaller groups that practical truth best penetrates into daily life. Jesus spent half His ministry life with twelve individuals, and then special times with three among those twelve (who would have the amazing privilege of writing some of the New Testament Scriptures). How does our activity measure up to that?

It has been my observation over the years that those who include effective small group interaction in their spiritual walk exhibit the greatest degree of transformational living, over those who neglect this aspect.

Debi and I have led or participated in many small groups through several denominations and have found one versatile format highly effective when led by properly gifted leaders. We learned about it from the Cell Church movement, termed the four W's: Welcome (man to man), Worship (man to God), Word (God to man) and Works (God through man).

The *Welcome* is a wonderful time of connecting with real lives. A true disciple genuinely loves and cares about those around him. As the gathering unfolds, there is general conversation about what has been happening in each other's lives, good and bad. People feel loved and valued, and confidentiality is maintained among the members.

At some point, attention is turned toward God in *Worship*. As worship commences, the affairs of daily living fall away, and He gets our special focus. Worship can be any combination of things that draw us to give Him pre-eminence in the group. It could be prayer, singing, a poem, a God story, silence, etc.

Once He has our full attention, the *Word* is brought to bear upon each member, as God speaks to us the things of eternal importance to Him. This could be a verse discussed, a Scripture pertaining to an issue an individual is facing, a teaching (although we have found mini-sermons to be less effective here), with interaction about what has been taught, a longer reading of His Word, etc.

Lastly, once teaching has been internalized, a final discussion takes place regarding how we will be responding to what was received. These *Works* may take the form of specific steps, a plan for implementation in a particular circumstance, a general procedure for all, or even a group task.

The important ingredient here is the consecration of our lives, and the integration of His truth through us to the surrounding culture. Throughout the evening, the 'one anothers' are also given freedom to operate, as the Spirit of God leads.

The Church would be so powerful in this world if we daily engaged with one another for what we could GIVE rather than for what we could GET! Tragically, much of our 'gathering' for church has become an assembly of individuals seeking to be entertained by a great concert-like worship band, a theatre-style soloist and a conference-style preacher in a nightclub-style setting. And we should be shamed by our own 'post-game' comments! "Well, that wasn't one of the pastor's better sermons." "I didn't like that first song, and Julie was out of tune." "I wish we could get rid of those drums, the music was so loud this morning." "The message was 12 minutes overtime! We'll never get a table at Swiss Chalet now!"

Church is not primarily a physical act, but a spiritual celebration of the relationship between the saints and Almighty God, through the precious blood of Christ in the power of the Holy Spirit. Jesus cleansed the temple of 'robbers' who misused the gathering place for earthly, fleshly self-motivated goals. He proclaimed His House as "A HOUSE OF PRAYER" (Matthew 21:13)! Our fellowship is intended to prayerfully draw each other closer to Christ and inspire the elevation of our passion to serve Him.

Worship

I barely know what to write here, honestly. How can I express HIS WORTH in mere words! What I want to say here is that worship is offering Him what He deserves, not what we desire, but that is not enough. I'd like to offer that worship should express our full love for Him, while offering our full submission to Him; still not sufficient! What we do, say and sing is not worship. These are merely the 'expressions', simplistic tools for our worship. To me, worship is putting us both in our proper postures. In every way that He gives me strength and insight to do so, I exalt Him above all else, while taking the stance of complete humility within my own soul, before His mighty Throne; nope, I can't properly express it.

Let me offer some Scripture instead. After the rebuilding of the Temple in Nehemiah's day, Ezra called all the people to reinstitute the worship of God in Jerusalem.

> *"And Ezra opened the book in the sight of all the people for he was standing above all the people; and when he opened it, all the people stood up. Then Ezra blessed the LORD the great God. And all the people answered, "Amen, Amen!" while lifting up*

their hands; then they bowed low and worshiped the LORD with their faces to the ground."   Nehemiah 8:5-6

Well, that is getting better. You see, standing up, and lifting hands, and bowing low, face to the ground are great expressions of a heart of reverence and humility toward our majestic Creator and Abba Father.

Psalm 99 recites,

"The LORD reigns, let the peoples tremble; He is enthroned above the cherubim, let the earth shake! The LORD is great in Zion, and He is exalted above all the peoples. Let them praise Thy great and awesome name; Holy is He... Exalt the LORD our God, and worship at His footstool; Holy is He."   Verses 1-3, 5

You see, the intimacy of the love He is producing within your soul is meant to burst forth from your body in spirited and genuine expressions of worship!

How tragic when we enter the sanctuary, glued to our cell phones or engaged in worldly business conversation, rather than with hearts fully prepared to lift His Name. How glib we can be to go about our day complaining of all sorts of things, rather than enjoying His gracious Presence. 1 Thessalonians 5:16-18 reminds us: "Rejoice always; pray without ceasing; in everything give thanks; for this is God's will for you in Christ Jesus." How much better it is to

Enter His gates with thanksgiving, and His courts with praise. Give thanks to Him; bless His name. For the LORD is good; His lovingkindness is everlasting, and His faithfulness to all generations.   Psalm 100:4-5

Yes, now we are getting there!

Summary

Imagine a service where every saint enters having prepared themselves in prayer and fasting ahead of time; where each one brings an offering of spiritual readiness, and walks through the door of the sanctuary full of the Holy Presence of God to share with others. Imagine how different that service would be if the chairs were removed, and the floor was the major feature for the prayers of the saints, on bended knees! Imagine if two or three read from the Word and expounded the truth of Christ, with others commenting and extending the blessing of the Word of God

> *"for teaching, for reproof, for correction, for training in righteousness; that the man of God may be adequate, equipped for every good work."*   2 Timothy 3:16-17

Imagine the blessing for the congregation (sheep) if the elders fervently and spiritually guided and guarded them with the authority of the Holy Spirit, yanking them back from sin with the crooked staff of the shepherd, and admonishing them with the rod of truth.

To the extent that the Church conforms to the kingdom (Kingship) of God and not the secularization of its structure and procedure, to that degree will the Church transform the encompassing society. Living a biblical culture requires seeing the church as the body of His beloved, instituted by Jesus Himself, and never to be neglected. The disciple of Christ takes on the stance of Paul, who declared,

> *"And we proclaim Him, admonishing every man and teaching every man with all wisdom, that we may present every man complete in Christ. And for this purpose also I labor, striving according to His power, which mightily works within me."* Colossians 1:28-29

Each of us is commanded to use our unique set of spiritual gifts for the edification of the body of Christ, and the culture around us. When we gather for what each of us can spiritually contribute, the transformational power of the church will be felt throughout whatever secular society we inhabit!

MUSIC

*Much of the lyrical content
has moved from expressions
of total obedience, to
songs of spiritual need,
and then further, to
songs of praise and worship.*

I have seen in my lifetime the encroachment of human culture into the church, as many of His people further enculturate themselves into the world of entertainment, technology and frivolous distractions. The drift from living out a biblical culture is even exemplified in the content of church songs over my lifetime. Much of the lyrical content has moved from expressions of total obedience: *'Trust and Obey'*, 'for there's no other way', to songs of spiritual need, like *'Create in Me a Clean Heart'* and then further, to songs of praise and worship: *'How Great is Our God'*.

Worship and praise, of course, are the easiest to sing with passion because God always comes through and does His part. We can readily jump up and down and praise Him for all He has done for us, because it does not require responsive obedient living. For a growing number, obedient service and transformational living are become too difficult a pursuit in these darkening days, so we sing less about 'our part' now, and more about His.

In the days of my youth much of the lyrical orientation in church music stemmed from the Hymns. There seemed to be a much more focused emphasis on *service*. Songs like, *'I'm in the Lord's Army'* gave me the image of committed soldiers, marching in step with and for Jesus.

The impression in my mind was of a unified body of disciples, living and marching together in harmony, with Jesus out front leading the charge against sin, and opening the pathway to heaven! *'I Surrender All'* was sung with passion and tears, and we meant every word of it... and we worked relentlessly on living transformed lives. "I will go anywhere and do anything for my Master." "I will obey His Voice."

Since those days, I have observed two major shifts from this, represented in much of the music of the Church. The first major transition in the church changed the question from "How can I know God's Will?" to "Can I do this 'behaviour' and still be a Christian?" The slide seemed to develop during the latter stages of the 'Jesus Movement', after the resistant Church received and accepted the Hippie Christians, with their focus on peace and love and 'simply worship Jesus'. The new musical styles began to express these sentiments, and the service orientation of church music was transformed into worship of the Trinity.

'Awesome God' is a prime example of this first transition. *'Our God is an awesome God'* was followed by a list of His supernatural abilities. Raised hands emerged as the symbol of this worship, and the main person sought after by a church planter became a *drummer*. In those days Keith Green lamented the *established* churches being *'Asleep in the Light'*.

I remember candidating for a Youth Pastor position in 1985 at a church in British Columbia. One of the laments I expressed to the congregation at that time was that churches seemed more interested in acquiring a drummer than saving a soul. Interestingly, I was told in a phone call a few weeks later that it had come down to myself and one other candidate. They expressed that they really wanted me, but they had chosen the other candidate because he was from California, had blond hair, and they thought the young people would find that 'cool'... a sign of the times for the '80's.

Since then, more *modern* music penetrated most churches, and full scale bands became the norm. Personally, I loved the musical shift, but more and more the lyrics departed from the detailing of service *for* Jesus to praise *of* Him.

CHURCH MUSIC HISTORICAL CHART

Lyrical Orientation	Song Examples	Church Planter Priority
Service-oriented	I'm in The Lord's Army Trust and Obey I Surrender All	Evangelist
Worship-oriented	Awesome God	Drummer
WARNING	Asleep in The Light	
Self-oriented	Rain Down/Heal Me Answer my Prayers	Projector/Laptop/ Sound system
WARNING	Does Anybody Hear Her?	

But now I have seen a second shift, which causes even greater concern within my soul. There seems to be a new orientation toward songs expressing what HE does for ME! This new lyrical sign of the times seems so *natural* as we sing, but must be so grievous to the Father. We are becoming so self-oriented that we seldom even notice the needs around us. Rather poignant, is the song '*Does Anybody Hear Her?*' by *Casting Crowns*.

Nothing against the composers, mind you, it is just a further sign of decay from walking out a biblical culture in a secularizing world. Now the main sought after features for a church planter are a *projector*, a *laptop* and a *$100,000 sound system*!

From organs to drums to images, we progress toward the end of this dying world, thinking less of following Jesus and more of receiving from Him, with everyone 'doing what was right in his own eyes'.

I know I sound pretty pessimistic here, but I am merely trying to point to generalized trends. There are many churches out there doing spiritually transformative things musically, but sometimes the job of a leader is to forecast the spiritual darkening of a generation, and that is what I am observing.

LEADERSHIP

*Elders are meant
to 'guard and guide',
not 'dictate and decide'.*

*If your church has men among you
to appoint leaders from,
who live a biblical culture,
then you will love your church
and be truly blessed
by their watchful care
and guidance over you.*

As I mentioned earlier, each local church needs a plurality of spiritual leaders. A single leader is inadequate at best, and potentially a real detriment to a congregation. Wherever I have seen a single leader, the church demonstrates strength where he has strong gifts, and weakness where he does not. A plurality of leaders better ensures a gift mix covering all the strengths needed to provide spiritual leadership under the authority of the Head of the church, Jesus Christ.

"Let the elders who rule well be considered worthy of double honor, especially those who work hard at preaching and teaching."   1 Timothy 5:17

Implied in this passage is a multiplicity of spiritual leaders, who function diligently and honourably as the 'elders' of the church.

Elders

Without elders, a church body cannot function properly in the spiritual realm. To those who insist elders are not necessary, or use alternate systems of governance, I repeat, "Why would God place a list of qualifications for elders in His Word, if we were not meant to have them?" After the Apostle Paul preached the gospel in a city and disciples were formed, they

"appointed elders for them in every church, having prayed with fasting, they commended them to the Lord in whom they had believed." Acts 14:23

The elders 'job' is to attend to the spiritual matters in regard to the congregation, NOT to choose carpet colours or direct any other of the many and varied temporal affairs of the church. I have often commented that elders are meant to 'guard and guide', NOT 'dictate and decide'! Elders get in trouble when they begin to autocratically 'rule', dictating orders. 1 Peter 5:2-3 advises,

"shepherd the flock of God among you... not for sordid gain... nor yet as lording it over those allotted to your charge, but proving to be examples to the flock."

When faced with an administrative complaint, Paul responded,

"It is not desirable for us to neglect the word of God in order to serve tables. But select from among you, brethren, seven men of good reputation, full of the Spirit and of wisdom, whom we may put in charge of this task. But we will devote ourselves to prayer, and to the ministry of the word." Acts 6:2b-4

Deacons are tasked with the leadership of the daily temporal matters of the church, a duty just as burdensome a spiritual responsibility as eldering (see 1 Timothy 3:8-10, 12-13). Both offices bear the load of exemplary personal godly living and an accompanying reputation in the fellowship of true believers, and in the community at large.

Elders are responsible for 'guarding the flock'. Paul warned the elders of the church in Ephesus,

> *"Be on guard for yourselves and for all the flock, among which the Holy Spirit has made you overseers, to shepherd the church of God which He purchased with his own blood. I know that after my departure savage wolves will come in among you, not sparing the flock; and from among your own selves men will arise, speaking perverse things, to draw away the disciples after them."*   Acts 20:28-29

Sadly, even among the leaders are those whose words will deceive, stir up trouble, bring false teaching and all manner of mischief, to stroke their pride and gain some power (review Matthew 23:2-33 for leadership *red flags*). This is another strong case for a plurality of leadership; to avoid one person leading the congregation astray.

Guarding means having the Spirit's discernment over things which are spiritually false or deceptive, even among the eldership. We have three enemies; the world, the flesh and the devil. We also have three overcoming allies; the Father, the Son and the Holy Spirit. In order to guard the flock against the three enemies, an elder must not place much value in possessions, passions or pride, but have the genuine heart of God for the people. He must remain alert, and guard himself against "the lust of the flesh, and the lust of the eyes and the boastful pride of life" (1 John 2:16). To the extent he is successful over the course of a day, is the degree to which He will be able to be used by God to effectively guard others in the fellowship He is given to oversee.

Guiding is another elder role. Elders must have the ability, under the grace of our Lord, to not only guard against wrong spiritual directions, but to provide correct godly direction. The list of elder qualifications (see Titus 1:5-9 and 1 Timothy 3:1-7) help ensure your elders will model those directions by godly personal lives. Both lists basically outline a sacrificial denying of self, being alive to Christ, and having accompanying leadership qualities.

When it comes to being a *preaching* elder, be cautious of those who say they 'love preaching'. A preaching elder must 'love the PEOPLE' he is preaching to, but bear the preaching responsibility as a spiritual burden; "Let not many *of you* become teachers, my brethren, knowing that as such we shall incur a stricter judgment" (James 3:1). Preaching (guiding publicly) is not being a *big personality*, a *popular person* or a *fluid entertainer*; it is being "a workman, who does not need to be ashamed, handling accurately the word of truth" (2 Timothy 2:15).

What set Jesus apart from the rest was that He spoke *unlike* any of the others. People were amazed at the power and authority of his words! (See Matthew 7:28-29) That kind of preaching can only occur when there is a direct connection with the Father through the Holy Spirit. This is why some pastoral messages effect change in people's hearts and others just pass right by. Even those dull of hearing either opposed or responded to Jesus when He spoke; very few remained neutral.

Now I am sure by now you have noticed I use 'him' regarding an elder and a deacon. I do so carefully and intentionally. This has become a thorny issue throughout the church, but I do want to give an opinion on why I believe elders and deacons are to be men and not women. This is an area which must not be discussed using deceptively current 'cultural' values, since the times are never to be trusted in purely spiritual matters.

I believe we must go right back to Genesis and consider Adam and Eve. Both of them received separate and distinct 'punishments' for their first sinful actions. If we review Eve's 'consequences', it included subservience to a male. This was not because the male was smarter, a better leader, more gifted, preferred or anything of the sort. It was simply the consequential choice of the Father, given the manner by which she gave herself over to sin.

If you look carefully in Genesis 3:6, Eve succumbed to sin in three ways. First, she sinned by the *lust of her flesh*: "when the woman saw that that the tree was good for food", then *lust of the eyes*: "and that it was a delight to the eyes", and also the *boastful pride of life*: "and that the tree was desirable to make *one* wise". Even Paul refers to this when he says, "And *it was* not Adam *who* was deceived, but the woman being quite deceived, fell into transgression" (1 Timothy 2:14). The consequence of Eve being 'quite deceived' was a removal of her from the decision-making responsibilities of spiritual leadership.

We speak in theological circles about the imputation of Adam's sin upon all of mankind. But here it speaks of the imputation of Eve's sin upon women. Her consequence led to the subservient nature of womankind within a marriage and within the church structure. There is no value or warrant in comparing males with females in this regard. Nor do I believe God would have put 'male leadership' in Scriptural motion, if it was simply a 'cultural thing' for Paul's day. In fact, it has nothing whatsoever to do with males in leadership. It is simply the choice of God, as He gave this consequence for Eve's volitional and emotional fall from grace. It is something women since that day have had to 'bear' as a result.

Men have their own cross to bear from the fall, and it would serve the church better to 'bear one another's burdens', help each other live gracefully within the confines of these consequences, and not engage in useless comparative argumentation.

Let me just add that if your church has men among you to appoint leaders from, who do live a biblical culture, then you will love your church and be truly blessed by their watchful care and guidance over you. Make sure you give them "double honor" (1 Timothy 5:17).

It is also vital to rise up young male disciples, who love the Lord, and will eventually fill these terribly responsible positions. For those aspiring to eldership, "it is a fine work he desires to do" (1 Timothy 3:1b). But do not place them in position too early; "not a new convert, lest he become conceited and fall into the condemnation incurred by the devil" (1 Timothy 3:6). If neglected, your church women will lament the lack of men able or willing to lead, and may be unwisely tempted to fill these roles of leadership themselves, against the intentions of God.

Shepherding

One of the beautiful pictures given for an elder's tough and tender responsibility toward the church is that of a shepherd with his flock. Acts 20:28-31a reads,

> *"Be on guard for yourselves and for all the flock, among which the Holy Spirit has made you overseers, to shepherd the church of God which He purchased with His own blood."*

This is a pastoral role among the eldership, and demands careful spiritual attention to the members.

One day as I was reading through Zechariah I came upon a passage where God is scolding the 'foolish shepherds' of Israel, who were no longer fulfilling their role. Within this passage, is revealed an amazing synopsis of what the duties of the shepherd really are. Zechariah 11:16 lists these four elements:

care for the perishing,

seek the scattered,

heal the broken, or [and]

sustain the one standing.

Imagine the spiritual impact elders could have, if they built spiritual church *programs* around these four elements!

Evangelism is not about church growth, not about getting more people in to increase the budget, nor about being spiritually *successful*. It is about the first two elements, and some of the third on this list. We are to *care for the perishing*, not condemn them. That is, we are to offer true care for the ungodly. This sounds a lot like Christ's mandate: "For while we were still helpless, at the right time Christ died for the ungodly" (Romans 5:6). Caring means going to those outside God's family, listening genuinely, assisting practically, and sharing effectively; being the hands and mouth of Christ in their lives with great compassion and love. Some will respond, some will not; some will thank you, some will persecute you. Their response is not our focus, *caring* is.

For others who have been hurt by 'church' for whatever reason and have scattered from it, they are to be *sought out*, found, and restored "in a spirit of gentleness" (Galatians 6:1b). Shepherds are called to leave the ninety nine of the flock "and go and search for the one that is straying" (Matthew 18:12b).

Many also are 'broken' by a combination of their own sinfulness and the sins of others. Regardless, the healing is the priority, not the blame. To *heal the broken* means to introduce them to the amazing grace and mercy of God, through His Son, in the power of the Spirit. It means to unfold the truth of His word to them in such a way as to restore them from the bondage of brokenness and sin, to the freedom of the healing arms of the Saviour.

Lastly (and we neglect this one most of all), to *sustain* the one standing. The applicable saying here is: 'the squeaky wheel gets the grease'. Often the most overlooked person in need of spiritual nourishment and encouragement is the one who appears to be fine in every respect. If those standing firm as pillars in the church begin to crumble, how will the rest be encouraged to likewise stand fast? Let's make sure we pray for the exemplary disciples among us, encourage them regularly, and convey especially to our leaders every aspect of what we appreciate about them.

Let me share a memorable illustration of some of these four elements in actions. One of the young men of our church found a great soul mate within our congregation, and married her. Uncertain and confused about his self-worth, he was tempted away by another woman. As leaders, we could have grieved for his wife and spoken evil of him.

Instead, we recommended his wife hold out the possibility of forgiveness, and went after the young man. We brought him in, shared the depth of God's love for him and the value we all placed upon him, and in shame and repentance he humbly turned back to his wife. She determined, under God, to give him another chance. Today, years later, he is pastoring a church, with a supportive wife and three tremendous children. Recently, his 12 year old daughter left this note for him in his office Sunday morning before he delivered God's Word. "Dear Daddy! I am so happy that you're a pastor!!! Everyone in our family is happy you're a pastor! (smiley face) May God bless you in mighty ways! I pray that God will be with you as you teach FBC about what it means to live sacrificially. (heart; cross) Love Sarah". Now there is a young girl who knows how to 'sustain the one standing'!!!

MENTORING

To me, a spiritual mentor is
someone whose personal
quest for truth, found in Jesus,
has been sufficiently translated
into a Spirit-led lifestyle
so as to inspire another
of the value and direction
of that quest.

I wanted to reserve a section just to share a little more of my own personal spiritual journey, by recounting some of my 'mentors'. To me, a spiritual mentor is someone whose personal quest for truth, found in Jesus, has been sufficiently translated into a Spirit-led lifestyle so as to inspire another of the value and direction of that quest. In His great orchestration of my own life, God provided mentors, both near and far to keep me propelled toward godliness. I cannot mention all of the positive influences He placed around me, for God's ways of influence are beyond measure and staggering in complexity. He deals with nations and at the same time touches each of our hearts intimately and personally.

Earlier on, I mentioned a few individuals close at hand, but here I want to outline a few broader mentors, mostly musicians. God saw fit for me to grow up during the decade of the "Jesus People" movement in North America. Confused by seemingly senseless wars and a lack of meaning behind mundane industrialization, the hippie movement of peace and love spawned a quest for truth and meaning that, for many, led to the discovery of Jesus Christ. His ageless offer of 'salvation' from sin and death propelled many drug cultured youth into a new life of Spirit-led devotion to God, through the message of the cross.

Largely shunned by the established church culture of the day, these newly converted hippies searched for anyone versed in the Bible who seemed to be able to convert the message into a life of spiritual purpose. One of the more prominent places of discovery was in a little church called 'Calvary Chapel' in California, led by Pastor Chuck Smith. I mention this, not because I was personally involved with it, but because of certain people whose relationships developed there, which led to enormous impact upon my young life through their music and lyrics.

I think the earliest of these mentors was Larry Norman, called by many the 'father' of Christian rock music. From the age of five Larry Norman was unequivocally and unapologetically in love with Jesus. What impacted me most from his life and music was the confident and intelligent approach he displayed with the people on the street who were damaged, and searching in many of the 'wrong' places for truth and meaning. He boldly spoke of unmentionable or delicate topics like gonorrhoea, the immoral nature of judgment and condemnation within much of the suburban church culture, and the usefulness of 'good' rock music to speak of Jesus. He made me want to be more than a church goer; to have a higher level of devotion than Sunday church, and to be unashamed of Jesus Christ out in the marketplace.

Larry's 1972 album '*Only Visiting This Planet*', which I purchased in my second year as a young Christian, has been regarded as one of the top contemporary Christian music albums of all time. It is a 'must listen to' in my estimation, even to this day. His later (1976) '*In Another Land*' recording further convicted me to hold lightly the things of this world, and live my life with allegiance only to the kingdom (Kingship) of God.

Through his influence, we enthusiastically dyed the imprint of his 'One Way Jesus' hand symbol onto white T-shirts, and boldly wore them in our high school and around town. In my Bible College days I often argued in the College President's office, like Larry, against the 'politics' of the institution. In the summers while working out in the mountain tourist town of Banff, Alberta I launched and managed "The Fireplace" Coffeehouse as a venue to stir up conversations about Jesus among the *backpack traveller* crowd. My commitment was solely for His use, and never to take a 'summer holiday' from the Lord.

Another mentor of mine, Keith Green, became connected to Larry through a mutual friendship with Randy Stonehill. While Randy was the 'Barnabas' to Larry, the 'Paul', he was also the 'Joshua' to Keith, the 'Moses'. I highly recommend taking a well spent hour of time watching the You Tube video: *The Keith Green Story (Full)*. Keith followed his own path with the Saviour. His 1977 album '*For Him Who Has Ears to Hear*' was pivotal in my life.

His growing and infectious passion for Jesus, and vocal disdain for all things 'nominal' in the church, launched me ahead (like the slingshot bar to a pinball). His penetrating lyrics stimulated my own spiritual passion toward a *no compromise* lifestyle; 'dying to self' and being 'alive to Christ', regardless of the lure from the world, the flesh or the devil. I can picture him, and recall myself reading Luke 6:46-49 for the first time, "And why do you call me 'Lord', 'Lord' but do not do what I say?", followed by outlining the dangers of a 'house built on sand' and washed away in troubled times from a lack of zeal for obedience to Christ.

Partially in response to these mentors, on October 29th of 1974 I made the first of only two life vows to the Lord (the second being my life commitment to be joined in marriage with my precious wife, Debi). Whisked into my first year of University life, I quickly became aware that my commitment to Jesus would waiver and potentially fall if I did not hold fast to Him. So on that decisive evening I vowed before God to regularly be in His Word and under His influence for the rest of my life. From that day forward, I can count on one hand the number of times I have missed starting my day in His Word and before His throne... now 40 plus years and counting.

Other mentoring influences included mostly musicians. Randy Stonehill demonstrated the beauty of deep friendships with his fun-loving '*Welcome to Paradise*' in 1976. The Second Chapter of Acts declared the majesty and power of God in their inspiring 1978 album '*Mansion Builder*'. Even the more mainstream musical group, the Imperials inspired me with their victory cries in 1979, with '*One More Song for You*'.

It continues to amaze me how God orchestrated a young budding musician, turned Pastor such as myself to have such an awe-inspiring influx of musical and spirit-oriented talent thrown into the mix of my life at such crucial points of my development as a discipler for Jesus!

I cannot conclude this section, however without mentioning Billy Graham. I shed some tears at the passing of Keith Green on July 28th of 1982. I shed some more when Larry left this planet on February 24th of 2008 and I know I will shed some more at the conclusion of Billy's earthly life. His influence guided me by shining example through the days of 'celebrity' pastors falling headlong into mentor-damaging sinfulness.

As I write this, Billy has recently introduced his *final message* of hope and salvation to the world in his 90th year of life. Similar to the days of Josiah, where God held back the tide of sin, I personally believe God has once again held back a nation from darkening days for a whole generation so Mr. Graham could complete the ministry God called him to, and the role He played for the 'kings' of the American and world landscape. Now the dam is breaking, and we will need to fortify our children's generation for the firestorm ahead.

DENOMINATIONS

We can no longer afford to be separated.
Now are the 'darkening days'
when mankind opposes us,
and the resulting persecution
will become the litmus test
for the true Church
of His disciples again.

God has taken me on quite an eclectic journey through a number of denominations, each of them displaying both strengths and weaknesses. For a short time my parents took us to a United Church. Though I was quite young, it seemed to me that this group had respect for God and were very organized. We jokingly called them the 'United Organization'. I came to faith in Jesus while attending a Baptist church for all the wrong reasons. While there, I found them to be very genuine, and concerned for my salvation. They were very nice to me, but seemed reluctant to answer my many questions. I 'landed' and grew in my faith at a Brethren Assembly. Here I found people of great intimacy with God, having a wealth of biblical understanding and a willingness to carefully share it with me.

In our first years of marriage, Debi and I attended and ministered within an A.G.C. Church (Associated Gospel Church). They were quite solid people and represented well the conservative evangelical stream. After returning from some mission work in England and Kenya, we served in a First Regular Baptist group. They were indeed very 'regular' and orderly, and we were warmly welcomed into His service there. We next 'planted' a church in Canmore, Alberta, again under the umbrella of the A.G.C..

Moving to the East coast of Canada, after four years of teaching at Briercrest Bible College, we were called to lead a Mennonite Brethren congregation. These folks proved quite alive and vibrant spiritually, and seemed to incorporate more of the Spirit in their worship and conversation. For a number of years I provided leadership at a church associated with the C&MA (Christian and Missionary Alliance). I found them to be quite evangelistic, emphasizing numeric growth and offering a climate of 'whomsoever will may come' to their services.

Receiving a call back to western Canada, I pastored a Mennonite group, who were very 'proper' in their respect for God and quite loyal to their European Anabaptist roots and culture. Now in Roatan, Honduras we have been attending a Church of God, Pentecostal. This predominantly black islander group is genuinely lively, loud and excited, having great freedom in worship and offering passionate confession of sins.

As you can see, my experience with denominations has been rather expansive over the years. As a lover of Christ, it has long been a lament of mine to notice among denominationalism the tendency toward an imbalance of emphasis toward the Trinity. This has caused all manner of deception and division among the churches.

The 'mainline' churches have historically tended to emphasize *God*, believing in Him as Creator and Sustainer, and promoting the value of being an upstanding citizen in the community. The 'conservative evangelical' traditions seem to focus their primary allegiance on *Jesus*, valuing His Word, baptism, witnessing and a disciplined lifestyle. The 'Pentecostal' denominations expend much effort promoting the *Holy Spirit*, valuing experience and the pursuit of supernatural gifts and events.

Each tradition over the years has championed their own cause, and bemoaned the inadequacies of the others. The effect has been that each of the three denominational traditions is "holding to a form of godliness, although they have denied its power" (2 Timothy 3:5).

How much more biblically effective churches would become, if they expended their efforts 'responding' to all three Persons of the Trinity in an equally balanced manner! Such variety in worship, such power in exhortation, such effective witness, such beauty in community, such holiness of fellowship, such provision for truly 'stimulating one another to love and good deeds' (Hebrews 10:24b) this would engender.

Happily, this is what we are beginning to see emerging through the more independent *community* churches. As people search for a local church they can *relate to*, church planters are responding with ever more balanced approaches, incorporating all three wonderful Personalities of the Father, Son and Holy Spirit. Lively worship, solid teaching and a deep reverence for God are being presented as equally necessary and wonderful!

There has been a desperate need for the 'Church' to unite, and it seems like now is the time God Himself is bringing it to pass.

Thankfully, diminishing is the need for the era of denominationalism. Gone are the days when taking a stand against a corrupt church led to a denomination of people springing forth in defiance against culturally infected leadership (although that still exists to this day). Coming are the days of two choices; sheep or goats, in or out, for the Godhead or against Him. Ahead are the days when all the cultures of the world will rise up against His Church. We can no longer afford to be separated. Now are the 'darkening days' when mankind opposes us, and the resulting persecution will become the litmus test for the true Church of His disciples again. Let us together now, more than ever, find the appropriate balance of worship, exhortation, service and witness to draw us as the 'Bride of Christ' to holiness and readiness for His coming to take us home!

On the more negative side, I have observed two things deceptively creeping into the new church culture rather simultaneously, though perhaps not coincidentally. First, in wealthier cultures especially, the growing onslaught of reality TV shows and the increase in movie-going have caused an unconscious shift in expectations for church services to be *entertaining*.

No longer able to 'hold' congregational numbers by denominational loyalty, these new *community* churches are attracting large numbers of church-goers from all backgrounds, by strategically providing professionally orchestrated and highly entertaining gatherings. Now I am not being critical here, merely observing a major shifting trend in the culture of the gathered church.

In these gatherings, services are scripted to the second by technical geniuses. Children are effectively removed to playland palaces rivalling Disney World. Worship resembles the experience of a stadium concert. Visitors are whisked seamlessly from their vehicles to the choicest of seating.

The 'lead' pastor amazes us with poignant, hard-hitting, truthful messages delivered in a disarmingly entertaining manner, similar to a bestselling novelist. I liken the appeal of attending a service to taking in the weekly episode of your favourite TV series or movie sequel. And even if your church doesn't have the privilege of one of these phenomenal speakers, their messages are a mere Podcast away!

Given this high level of dedication to the service of God's Kingdom, one would think global revival would be imminent! I have observed the contrary.

This is due to a second related negative influence, the TV remote syndrome. We do not need to 'respond' to television shows or movies. We are shown how to survive in Alaska or on a desert island. We know how to get to deep space or the earth's core to save the world.

We become James Bondish and thwart the evildoers, or with invincible powers rescue our friends from certain death.

But what do we actually 'do' when the show is over? Certainly none of the things we just *observed*. When the show is over, we click the remote, turn it off, set it aside, and walk away unaffected, to the next event.

How tragically this mentality has subconsciously invaded the church service. How do we respond to a spiritually uplifting service? I put forth that media has taught us to turn off the button and forget about what has just been delivered to us. James prophetically described it this way:

"For if anyone is a hearer of the word and not a doer, he is like a man who looks at his natural face in a mirror; for once he has looked at himself and gone away, he has immediately forgotten what kind of person he was." James 1:23-24

What a waste of gifting and talent poured into all of those church services, meant to motivate a people of God's own possession, who leave it all in the sanctuary as they walk out the door. I pray you are not among their number.

Instead, I implore you to create or participate in groups of fellow Christians who come together and discuss the ways you can respond to what God's Spirit delivers to you on a weekly basis. Make sure you ingest spiritual food multiple times a day, both alone and around the table with others. Regardless of denomination or independence, make certain you pursue God, through His Son, in the power and guiding influence of the Spirit. Seek His truth above the traditions of man; "If possible, so far as it depends on you, be at peace with all men" (Romans 12:18). Expend little energy on divisive issues, and concentrate on 'loving your neighbour', and you will "enter into the joy of your Master" (Matthew 25:23b).

SERVICE

Everyone in the church
is meant to serve the Lord
in some capacity.
God, by His very design,
gifts some to speak
and others to serve,
and they are both doing
exactly what He
wants them to be doing!

From 1985-1990 the Lord had Debi and I 'plant' a church in Canmore, Alberta. We gathered in a senior's community hall, which meant setting up and taking down what we used every Sunday. During that period I overheard a few offhanded 'comments' from some, annoyed by others after the service. Some would be talking to people after the service and later remark, "Why do they need to remove the chairs right now. It's so noisy! Don't they care about evangelizing?" Those who were stacking chairs would equally exclaim, just loud enough for others to hear, "All they do is stand around talking while we do all the work!" I found this all rather comical, but unfortunate as well. It prompted a teaching on 'body life' in the church and how 'spiritual gifts' are meant to operate.

Everyone in the church is meant to serve the Lord in some capacity. God, by His very design, gifts some to speak and others to serve, and they are both doing exactly what He wants them to be doing! 1 Peter 4:10-11 explains,

"As each one has received a special gift, employ it in serving one another, as good stewards of the manifold grace of God. Whoever speaks, let him speak, as it were, the utterances of God; whoever serves, let him do so as by the strength which God supplies; so that in all things God may be glorified through Jesus Christ, to whom belongs the glory and dominion forever and ever. Amen."

Among the mix of several gifting strengths listed in Romans 12:6-8, they are divided into two 'kinds' of gifts here in 1 Peter as either the 'mouth' or the 'hands'. If you are a speaker type, then the mandate is to make sure you are speaking 'God stuff', so you will be spiritually influential to your culture. If, on the other hand, you are a server type, then your mandate is to help with 'God's strength', so you "do not grow weary of doing good" (2 Thessalonians 3:13b), and demonstrate godly service to your culture.

In terms of 'ministry', Scripture incorporates the image of a human body to portray how the members are to function together. Take time to read through the last half of 1 Corinthians 12 for a detailed explanation. Verse 17 offers an example of proper perspective when ministering together as a church; "If the whole body were an eye, where would the hearing be? If the whole were hearing, where would the sense of smell be?"

So when we collectively serve as a church body, the 'speakers' should pray a blessing on those who remove the chairs, enabling them to serve the Lord with their mouths. Similarly, the chair stackers ought to thank the Lord for those who are more gifted to share, while they perform their vital role with their hands... and all to the glory of God as each is uniquely gifted! Amen.

GIFTS

The third list, laid out for us in Romans 12:6-8
uses a more foundational Greek term,
'charisma', indicating these as gifts we possess,
built into our DNA at conception.

For much of my Christian experience I saw all the so-called 'spiritual gifts', mentioned in the New Testament, as one long list of 'possibilities'. We were told to pick the ones that seemed to describe us and then somehow understand what to do with them. Well, I thank God often for putting me on to a book written by Don and Katie Fortune, entitled *"Discover Your God-Given Gifts"*.[4] I recommend you order a copy and peruse it for yourself.

They really helped me better comprehend how we are meant to view the various gifts listed for us in 1 Corinthians, Ephesians and Romans. Three different Greek words were used to describe the types of gifts mentioned, but we translate all three simply as 'gifts'. The Greek audience would have known that very different things were being presented to them in each of these passages, and understood their distinctions.

The list of gifts put forth in 1 Corinthians 12:8-10 refer to the Greek word 'phanerosis', meaning a *manifestation*. They aptly termed these the 'Manifestation Gifts'. To me, this means these types of gifts are manifest through us at various points in time to cooperate with some activity God is engaged in. Verse 11 informs us that they are 'distributed as the Spirit wills'. So what this does NOT mean is we have these gifts within us to produce whenever we choose. They are not built in. They manifest through us when the Spirit chooses.

For example, I do not *possess* the 'word of wisdom' to bless others with as *my* gift. But as the Lord is using me to minister to someone, the Spirit may bless them with a 'word of wisdom' through me. This holds true with all of these manifestations, and especially cleared up for me the oft confusing use of 'tongues' and their interpretations. We are not meant to speak in unknown 'tongues' at will. Perhaps never, or a time or two, or on a regular basis the Spirit may give such an utterance through me "for the common good" (1 Corinthians 12:7).

To me, then, this precludes any notion that 'tongues' are a sign of salvation, a second filling or the like. It is up to the Spirit whether and when these kinds of gifts pour out through me, and not within my authority to command.

A second list, found in Ephesians 4:11, incorporates the Greek word 'doma', meaning *a present*. These 'Ministry Gifts', as termed by the Fortunes, are people gifts; presents from God given to a particular group of people for a specific season, to carry out the ongoing purposes of His Kingdom.

We are commanded to treat them with honour, to obey and submit to them, since "they keep watch over your souls" (Hebrews 13:17). In the process, we are also to beware of 'false prophets... wolves in sheep's clothing' (Matthew 7:15), the 'leaven of the Pharisees' (Luke 12:1b), etc. What a joy to gather and minister under the wisdom and leadership of godly elders, under-shepherds of the Head of the Church, Jesus Christ!

The third list, laid out for us in Romans 12:6-8 uses a more foundational Greek term, 'charisma', indicating these as gifts we *possess*, built into our DNA at conception. Each of us are commanded to be doing each of these things: perceiving, serving, teaching, exhorting, giving, administering and showing compassion. But since we are part of a larger body, some better as *hands* and others as *mouths*, God gives each of us a unique mixture of strengths and weakness among these 'possession' gifts, in order to live out our particular role within His Church. The Fortune's book includes a great tool of questions to help you discover your mix of strengths, and focus in on your most effective means of ministry within the church and among your surrounding culture.

I am strongest in perceiver (discernment), administration (leadership) and teaching. These gifts God has used through the professions of pastor, elder and missionary, which have occupied my life up to this point. Perhaps, writer can now be added to the list... Serving and compassion have been my weaker areas of ministry, so I have not given priority to these facets of ministry as *career* options.

By God's wisdom, a foot should be a foot and a hand a hand. This may seem ridiculously obvious when viewing parts of the human anatomy, but within the church family we see things like Sunday School teachers who are NOT gifted at teaching, yet accepted the position because of constant pleas of need from the pulpit. I believe we should have no ministry offered by the church that He has not first supplied the right gifted personnel to operate. I also fully trust that God will supply everything and everyone necessary to carry out the things He does call us to do.

Now my wife's strongest gifts are compassion (mercy) and discernment (perceiver). As a team we 'fit' together beautifully, and bear up each other's weaknesses with our strengths. Yes, she really does 'complete me'!

So when counselling, for instance, when a person comes to us broken, Debi is so gifted at empathizing and weeping with them. I sit back amazed at her ability to feel their pain and journey with them. When the tears subside and they get to the point of wanting advice on resolving their dilemma, I step in with an analysis of the situation and a healthy three point plan to proceed with. Together, we are much more effective than either of us could be alone. I believe it is actually by

God's design that 'opposites attract', for then one truly does complete the other when the two become one flesh.

So to recap, I do not go around proclaiming that "I possess the word of wisdom" for whoever might need it. However, as I continue to try living out a biblical culture each day, the Spirit may give me a 'word of wisdom' to encourage or exhort someone He is dealing with. What a 'gift' are those moments when we are permitted the glory of participating in a *God activity*.

Similarly, no one *possesses* the gift of Apostle or evangelist, but God may ordain them to such a task for a season, to benefit His eternal plan for His people, and this world He has placed us in.

But I can list with confidence my strong gift mix of perceiver/administrator/teacher he has uniquely endowed me with, which became 'spiritual' gifts when His Spirit entered me at the moment of my salvation. I can now incorporate these to serve His Kingdom for my generation.

ISSUES

It's not what you're against,
but Who you are for!

Our goal should be to
rescue people FROM the darkness,
not condemn them FOR their darkness.

One day, as I was struggling before God in prayer to understand the mind of Christ for one of our confusing and complex congregational 'issues', the Lord impressed this phrase upon my heart. It literally revolutionized our church and altered the course we were on, toward healing and more effective ministry. Here is what I received within my spirit: "It's not what you're against... but Who you are for!" This new motto gave us the courage and strength to quit all the arguing over what was 'wrong' with everybody and with the world around us, and to refocus our attention on declaring what was 'right' with the Trinity!

Christendom expends an inordinate amount of time and energy, often with great anger and agitation, serving causes that fight against evils in this world. I recall one organization which for years took on legal cases against immoral issues, most of which ultimately were not judged in their favour. This was inevitable from the outset, because the world does not want a biblical culture.

Romans 12 offers great insight here, regarding a *better* response. Yes, we must "Abhor what is evil, [and] cling to what is good" (verse9b), but the passage goes on to say, "Bless those who persecute you; bless and curse not" (verse 14) and then summarizes, "Do not be overcome by evil, but overcome evil with good" (verse 21b).

The Bible is also definitive about us not judging those outside the Christian faith 'for they are already judged' (see 1 Corinthians 5:12-13a). They already have eternal separation from God facing them, and that is punishment enough.

More time needs to be spent declaring 'Who' we are for. What should occupy most of our efforts is the demonstration of how we 'live in love with Jesus'. If we live our lives according to a truly biblical culture, it will most certainly become irresistibly attractive to some. But we must live in love with Jesus; really and truly in love with Him. We must love Him sufficiently that we daily grieve over our sins. This means we strive by His Spirit's strength and power not to live as close to worldly culture as we can, but as far from sin as possible.

This means personally following biblical directives on the same social issues we speak against. Our goal should be to rescue people from the darkness, not condemn them for their darkness.

When the church inordinately protests all of the issues disintegrating our culture from biblical foundations, it is paramount to declaring 'God is not in charge' of human history, and 'He doesn't know what He is doing!' If God permits a culture to increase in immoral activity, for His hidden overarching purposes to unfold, then why would we do otherwise?

Yes, we stand for what is right in God's eyes. Yes, we declare our allegiance to His Word on moral/social issues, but the bulk of our endeavours must be concentrated on demonstrating His love for those bound up in the ways of the world, the flesh and the devil.

Colossians 4:5 reads, "Conduct yourselves with wisdom toward outsiders, making the most of the opportunity". Further, "Let your speech always be with grace, seasoned, *as it were*, with salt, so that you may know how you should respond to each person" (verse 6). The only dilemma with this approach is the lack of 'good news' many believers have to share. How can we tell people the 'good news' of Jesus Christ if we are not personally experiencing the powerfully awesome impact of the Gospel in our own hearts and lives?

Watchmen Nee once wrote a little book called, "The Normal Christian Life".[5] In it he declared that an intimate relationship with Jesus, coupled by a lifestyle of radical discipleship, resulting in a powerful and effective ministry should actually be 'normal' for the church of God's people.

When we are closely connected with Jesus on a daily basis, we will have 'God stories' (as I love to call them) every day. We will have so many 'good news' experiences to share that they will overshadow any complaints we might have about the darkness around us. I believe more souls are saved by declaring the light of God than descrying the bad in the world.

What a force the church of Christ becomes when we join surrendered hearts together to let the world know how wonderfully joyful and meaningful life can be under the will of God, directed by Jesus Christ and passionately enlivened by the Holy Spirit.

CONFLICT

Hurt people, hurt people.

There are three sides to every story,
and God's is the only correct one!

People behave the way they do for a reason. I have often been helped by the reminder, 'hurt people hurt people'. When someone attacks another verbally, there is usually some underlying hurt within them causing the volatility of their response. The impulsive reaction is to argue back, stating your position firmly with lawyer-like precision. We usually presume that we are right, and being wronged. I have learned over the years to humbly accept that 'there are three sides to every story, and God's is the only correct one!'

Luke 6:27 offers instead, "But I say to you who hear, love your enemies, do good to those who hate you." There are always underlying issues that set people off; whether purposely or inadvertently, you have triggered something in them by a word, action or behaviour which has initiated their pain. That response comes from a source inside of them needing attention and repair.

I have found great benefit in taking a deeper interest in 'why' the person is railing against me. It is important to humbly lay aside my own feelings, and take the time to discuss why they are upset; genuinely caring about what has caused the conflict. By gaining an understanding of what is behind their action, it gives me greater ability to have real empathy for them. It sometimes even offers me the opportunity to participate in their healing process, and bring reconciliation.

The Bible says it better: "A gentle answer turns away wrath, but a harsh word stirs up anger" (Proverbs 15:1).

When the circumstances cannot be remedied, due to the other person's unwillingness, it sometimes feels like you are chained to the problem until they choose to forgive you, sometimes over years of time. I have found the illustration of the chain helpful for me. I picture two people in opposition to one another. There is a chain wrapped around both of their necks attaching them to one another, both of them feeling heavily weighed down by the issue. But at any point, I am free to take the chain off my own neck, whether the other person removes theirs or not. Through understanding, then empathy, and finally loving forgiveness, I do not need to remain tied to the conflict, waiting for their 'apology' or forgiveness.

Living a biblical culture does not let difficult life circumstances distract or hinder you from godly ministry. Ephesians 6:12 reminds us that

"our struggle is not against flesh and blood, but against the rulers, against the powers, against the world forces of this darkness, against the spiritual forces of wickedness in the heavenly places."

We fight a relentless battle against the devil, the enemy of our souls and his legions. The other human is NOT our enemy, just a fellow sinner, somehow caught in his trap of deceit. By remaining in a loving posture toward those agitated by us, God can work in their lives to turn them around; and our behaviour will either help or hinder that resolution.

There was a time when a powerful man in one of our churches became conflicted with me, my leadership and my person. In time the congregation began to feel the impact, and to suffer from it. Division and accusation began to arise and manifest, even through the influence of the enemy of our souls, beyond fleshly behaviour. As I wept in prayer over this, the Lord impressed upon me to stop opposing the criticism and instead endeavour to understand and love him. He directed me to go to the man's place of business and ask to pray with him on a weekly basis for a while. It was very difficult to obey, but with the conviction of the Holy Spirit I opened the door of that building and walked into I knew not what.

Fortunately, through the underlying faith and hidden heart of compassion the Spirit had placed within him, he could not refuse such an offer. I immediately began to pray for him, thanking God with a sincere heart for every good thing I had seen in and through him. I prayed a special blessing upon his family, his business and his life.

I believe it was mutual, hard to say, but I, at least began to enjoy and even savour those weekly times together in the presence and intimacy of God's throne. Needless to say, when God begins a good work He certainly establishes and accomplishes it. For the rest of his days this man's life was marked by a growing godliness, and he became more and more centered around helping the less fortunate both around him and around the world. His Christian leadership will not soon be forgotten!

SPLITS

*Simply put, they should not,
and need not happen... ever!

Let me say a word here about church splits. Simply put, they should not, and need not happen... ever! God permits them, for ultimately they 'root out the chaff from the wheat'. But like divorce, none of it is according to His intention; and 'woe to those' who cause them. Churches are meant to model Christian love and godly behaviour. Differences should be settled by godly elders who stick 'closer than a brother' in all circumstances. There is no problem God cannot resolve. There are only people unwilling to surrender their 'rights' for His greater purposes.

There is, in fact, a simple means of avoiding them. First of all, God is pretty firm in 1 Corinthians 6 against the extreme of lawsuits in the church. He laments,

> *"I say this to your shame. Is it so, that there is not among you one wise man who will be able to decide between his brethren, but brother goes to law with brother, and that before unbelievers? Actually, then, it is already a defeat for you, that you have lawsuits with one another. Why not rather be wronged?"*
> *Verses 5-7a*

Now in this passage it is implied that there should be at least one wise man among the group. It is also considered better to suffer a wrong than cause a split between brethren. So here is what can be done. Appoint a wise man (spiritually discerning) to go off alone on a retreat with the leaders of the church, to provide proper biblical perspective to the gathering. The leaders cannot return without having come to a resolution through prayer, fasting and spirit-led discussion. This resolution could solve the issue(s), or for one party to bow to the other and suffer wrong for the sake of the Kingdom. Regardless, it must be a unanimous resolution, to avoid further hidden conflict among the congregation.

Endless public and private meetings of sabre-rattling and shouting opposing views just polarize positions and disintegrate the trust of the people for their leadership. Essentially it is 'game over' early on, if spiritual discernment cannot quench the issue before it flares up. Whatever the conflict might be, the underlying issues are sinful disobedience that must be adequately rooted out and addressed by the godliest in your midst.

If it relates to a dispute based on opposing scriptural interpretations, allow the godly one(s) to come before His throne and choose one of the interpretations to follow first. If it is wrong, then let everyone repent and try the other one. I don't mean to be over simplistic here, but it really is just that straightforward. There is always a way ahead that does not split a congregation apart, if we are willing to set aside our selfish plans and let God direct the steps forward (Proverbs 16:9), even if we are the 'wronged' party along the way.

SUFFERING

Is it not a culturally human notion
that comfort and ease are better for us?

When I look at suffering from my own vantage point, it breaks my heart and makes no sense whatsoever that there is so much seemingly needless suffering in the world. And yet, through the lens of heaven it makes so much sense to me. The age old question arises in so many conversations, "How can a good God allow suffering in the world?" To me the answer is that God actually sent His only Son into the world to 'rescue us' from the eternal suffering caused by man's disobedience to Him, and from his accompanying sinful nature.

It is eternity that must be seen and understood, not temporal suffering in our brief stint on this planet. What gives us the notion that we were meant to live free from suffering? Is it not a culturally human notion that comfort and ease are better for us?

If God is all-knowing, and thus knows ahead of time that someone will never accept Him, and become eternally separated from Him, then in the larger picture, what does it really matter if his life ends at two years old or ninety; his end is the same. Conversely, if another is destined for heaven, what does it ultimately matter if he dies as an infant or lives to a ripe old age?

Now I hear you screaming how callous this sounds. Believe me, I know well the deep and lasting pain of losing loved ones tragically. But I say it this way to make the point that we are all created beings who live once, and briefly. So even as it pertains to suffering, to live a biblical culture means to accept that our lives are in His wonderfully capable hands. We serve His purposes in whatever way He sees fit, for whatever length of time He gives us.

It is by human culture alone that people demand to control their own temporal destiny, trying at all costs to avoid pain, and the many *inconvenient* consequences of their own sinfulness. That is why so many cultural 'issues' revolve around things like abortion, war, restricted freedom, and the like.

But the Bible notes,

"who are you, O man, who answers back to God? The thing molded will not say to the molder, "Why did you not make me like this," will it? Or does not the potter have a right over the clay, to make from the same lump one vessel for honorable use, and another for common use?" Romans 9:20-21

It is only human culture that drives people toward self-centeredness and selfish living. God graciously and continuously invites us toward 'the narrow way that leads to life' (Matthew 7:14), with Him in charge, ever for our best.

Now in everyday living, we all suffer consequences from our sins. Your mother tells you not to play with fire, but you disobey and end up burning your hand. Even if you are genuinely sorry for your actions, your hand is still burnt. We are told to forgive others who sin against us "up to seventy times seven" times (Matthew 18:22). Likewise, the Father forgives us when we repent and turn back from our sinful behaviours. Nevertheless, we suffer from the consequences.

A child results from a huge hormonal misstep in judgment, with everlasting consequences. A drunken man maims another for life from the accident he caused while driving home. Some suffering lingers in our regretful minds for years, even when fully forgiven. How much better it is to obey, and bypass the lasting pain of sin.

I see in Scripture that we also 'suffer for doing what is right' (1 Peter 2:20b). Jesus explains in John 15:20b, "If they persecuted Me, they will also persecute you". He adds in Matthew 5:10-12,

> *"Blessed are those who have been persecuted for the sake of righteousness, for theirs is the kingdom of heaven. Blessed are you when men cast insults at you, and persecute you, and say all kinds of evil against you falsely, on account of Me. Rejoice, and be glad, for your reward in heaven is great."*

This is the posture of a disciple, always viewing things through God's lens; the larger picture beyond the immediate circumstance. That is why we can receive the admonition: "love your enemies, and pray for those who persecute you" (Matthew 5:44).

Don't fall for the false teachings of the 'prosperity gospel' preachers, who tell you that you can have all the fame and fortune you want if your faith is just strong enough. Look carefully at all the 'heroes of faith' listed in Hebrews 11.

FAITH CHART
Results of living by faith – Hebrews 11:32-37

Power of His Resurrection	Fellowship of His suffering
by faith conquered kingdoms	others were tortured
performed acts of righteousness	others experienced mockings/scourgings
obtained promises	also chains and imprisonment
shut the mouths of lions	they were stoned
quenched the power of fire	they were sawn in two
escaped the edge of the sword	they were tempted
from weakness were made strong	they were put to death with the sword
became mighty in war	destitute/afflicted/ill-treated
put foreign armies to flight	wandered in deserts
received back dead by resurrection	living in caves and holes in the ground

You will see that several of them accomplished great things for God, even the miraculous, but several others suffered greatly. One experienced the miraculous, but another was sawn in two. Both had equally strong faith. One had temporal gain for God's kingdom; the other had temporary suffering and died a gruesome death for God's kingdom!

Now if both end up in heaven, free from all suffering, then why be so culturally bent on removing all brief suffering, discomfort, even inconvenience from our earthly life. Should we not rather live by faith for His kingdom activity and let Him choose the manner in which we receive suffering or blessing? I believe so. Look at Jesus' earthly life, and then ask yourself if we 'deserve' only prosperity!

1 Peter 3:13-17 aptly outlines the stance for those wanting to live a biblical culture here:

"And who is there to harm you if you prove zealous for what is good? But even if you should suffer for the sake of righteousness, you are blessed. AND DO NOT FEAR THEIR INTIMIDATION, AND DO NOT BE TROUBLED, but sanctify Christ as Lord in your hearts, always being ready to make a defense to everyone who asks you to give an account for the hope that is in you, yet with gentleness and reverence; and keep a good conscience so that in the thing in which you are slandered, those who revile your good behaviour in Christ may be put to shame. For it is better, if God should will it so, that you suffer for doing what is right rather than for doing what is wrong."

HEALING

*I hold that
healing occurs
when it serves
His purposes,
not our demands.*

Much of what has been said concerning suffering can be applied to healing as well. Matthew 8:16 states, that Jesus "healed all who were ill". He did so to physically demonstrate the spiritual reality of what Isaiah the prophet had spoken: "HE HIMSELF TOOK OUR INFIRMITIES, AND CARRIED AWAY OUR DISEASES" (verse 17).

We have got to get our minds off ourselves to achieve any grasp of what healing from Jesus is all about. It points to Him; it is all about Him, not the alleviation of our own pain, like some kind of 'party favours' from Jesus for being His follower. Yes, it was done sometimes out of shear compassion, out of the perfect love He had for us, but primarily it was done to instruct us on the significance and power of the cross He was about to bear... the sheer authority His death and resurrection would mean for each of us! It was all about Him!

For a disciple of Jesus, life is no longer about us at all... it is about seeking out His Kingdom activity and blending into it according to His will. Jesus heals to further the Kingdom work of His Father, not merely to free us from pain and suffering. The man born blind remained so for years, so Jesus could heal Him, and thereby demonstrate the power of God to a doubting group, giving them the opportunity to believe or deny.

Jesus does commend some for their faith, in the process of healing them, but it was not their faith that brought about their healing, it was His power. If our degree of faith could accomplish healing, then would we not, in essence, have the power to heal ourselves? We are told,

"For by grace you have been saved through faith; and that not of yourselves, it is the gift of God; not as a result of works, that no one should boast." Ephesians 2:8-9

I believe the 'concept' in this passage, relating to salvation, applies to healing, and all manner of things given solely by His grace and mercy toward us. Is it not this same 'boasting' attitude, which drapes the 'faith healers' in the stadiums?

I hold that healing occurs when it serves His purposes, not our demands. Yes, we can certainly petition Him to alleviate the physical and emotional pain and suffering we all experience in these temporal bodies. But this must be done in the same manner as Jesus, when facing the ultimate suffering of crucifixion; "My Father, if it is possible, let this cup pass from Me; yet not as I will, but as Thou wilt" (Matthew 26:39b).

TYPOLOGY

God gave physical examples
in the Old Testament
of spiritual realities
in the New Testament.

I have often referred to typology as 'physical examples in the Old Testament of spiritual realities in the New Testament'. I love them! I love how God has woven such beautiful portrayals together over thousands of years. Whether representative people, prophetic imagery or foreshadowing sacrificial procedures, they all point ahead to Christ, and what He would accomplish for our eternal redemption.

Some scholars warn against preaching Old Testament elements and stories as 'types' of Christ without New Testament verification that it was intended as such. They claim that if it is not explicitly explained in the New Testament, it is merely a potential *illustration* and not a *type*. I understand their caution and admire their devotion to accuracy. But when I see a picture in the Old Testament that seems to portray Christ, His Church or our salvation, it inspires me to greater faith in my Bible and a deeper love for the amazingly intricate nature of God. So, whether it is identified as a type or not, I would rather be inspired and wrong, than unaffected and right.

I see 'pictures' of Christ all over the Old Testament. Christ obviously did too, for after His resurrection, on the road to Emmaus, speaking to two disciples, Luke recounts,

"And beginning with Moses and with all the prophets, He explained to them the things concerning Himself in all the Scriptures." Luke 24:27

Now remember there were no New Testament Scriptures at this juncture.

Let me share a few examples here. The first would be considered a verifiable *type* of Christ. It can be viewed in Exodus 17, Numbers 20 and 1 Corinthians 10. After God's people were rescued from bondage in Egypt, they wandered through the desert on their way to the land already promised to them. When the people became thirsty they 'quarrelled' with Moses about it. God told Moses to 'take his staff, strike the rock and water would come out of it for the people to drink' (Exodus 17:5-6).

At a later stage of their journey, in the wilderness of Zin, they again 'contended' with Moses over the same need. This time God specified, "take the rod... and speak to the rock before your eyes, that it may yield its water" (Numbers 20:8a). Instead, Moses "struck the rock twice with his rod; and water came forth abundantly" (verse 11a). For his disobedience, God disqualified Moses from the joy of leading His people into the 'promised land', and he died out in the wilderness.

So what was so wrong with this little misdeed? It seems so unfair... unless you read 1 Corinthians 10:4: "all drank the same spiritual drink, for they were drinking from a spiritual rock which followed them, and the rock was Christ."

You see, it was a HUGE deal, because Moses unknowingly marred the physical picture of Christ, God intended for us in the church age. Christ was to be portrayed only ONCE being 'struck', symbolizing the once for all sufficient sacrifice of Himself on the cross, conquering sin and death. Thereafter, Christ would provide 'living water' by simply asking Him for it. So when Moses struck the rock a second time, after being told to speak to the rock, symbolically it was as if he was putting Christ on the cross again, portraying that His sacrifice for our sins once and for all, was insufficient.

For me, this indicates how important it is to follow His promptings in my own life without 'altering' them to suit myself. It warns me against slipping into a *routine* way of doing things, and missing the changes God might want me to make over time. It also stirs my soul with great joy to think that God had already destined Christ to conquer death, and provide my way back to Him even so many thousands of years ago! What a precious God I serve!

Let me share a second portrayal I have enjoyed, especially as it relates to my own worship. It is found in Ezekiel 46. In this passage each of the offerings and postures gives me personal and corporate (gathered for worship) analogous inspiration for my own actions of worship and obedience.

For example, in verse 2 the 'prince' enters first for worship and stands there while the priest offers burnt and fellowship offerings. In the Old Testament, the 'prince' refers to the coming Messiah, the "Prince of Peace" (Isaiah 9:6c). So, by analogy, Jesus enters first before His worshippers are permitted. The 'priest' is another emblem of Christ. The priest then offers burnt offerings. Leviticus clearly pictures Christ as making our way acceptable into God's holy Presence:

> *"If his offering is a burnt offering from the herd, he shall offer it, a male without defect; he shall offer it at the doorway of the tent of meeting, that he may be accepted before the Lord."*
> *Leviticus 1:3*

Amazing! Only after the burnt offering is made can the fellowship offering be provided, and that by the priest as well. For me this pictures me coming to worship God. The way is only open for me to be in

God's Presence because Christ's offering for my sin is first accepted by God in my stead. Then, and only then may I humbly enter the 'Holy of holies' and reverently bow prostrate before my God and offer my humble worship. It is here we together experience the depth of fellowship with heaven's *Author*.

WORSHIP CHART – EZEKIEL 46

A Biblical example from God's Levitical Temple

Scripture	Commentary
v1 east gate shut 6 working days/ open on 7th day	Spiritual battles of life six days/ 1 day devoted to gather for worship
v2 prince enters first/priest offers burnt and fellowship offerings	Jesus (Prince of peace) makes way possible to enter for worship
v2 gate left open for all until evening	Jesus opens way to worship through to end of devoted day
v3 people worship before the Lord	We have full access to worship in very Presence of God
v4 7th day prince offers 6 lambs/ one ram unblemished	6 days covered for spiritual living/7th day covered for freedom from labour
v5 ½ bushel grain offering with ram/ lambs with any amount grain	Jesus needed for worship offering/ offering amount by choice
v5 gallon olive oil for each ½ bushel grain offering	Properly prepared for worship
v6 new moon offering a young bull/ 6 lambs & 1 ram unblemished	Special occasion sin offering added for time of worship
v7 with lamb offerings, grain amount by choice/but proper oil amount	Our part allows for diversity of worship ability
v8 prince enters/exits same way	Jesus has no need of transformation by worship
v9 people must exit opposite way of entry	Worshippers need transformation/ leave different than arrival
v10 prince goes in and out among people	Jesus in midst whenever two or more gathered in His Name!
v11-12 prince gives personal offerings properly & gate is shut	The Perfect Lamb of God offered once for all!
v13 each day give year old lamb/ unblemished for a burnt offering	Remember every morning, our sin daily covered by Lamb of God
v14 grain offering each morning with proper mix of olive oil	Remember to worship Him every morning – 'My food is to do His will'!
v15 lamb every morning with grain offering & proper mix of oil	Jesus is ever present with me as I worship Him morning by morning!

Another visual example is in verses 8-9. Here we see the prince (Christ) entering and exiting the same way, while the worshippers must enter one way and exit the opposite way. I personally take this to mean HE needs no transformation before the Father, but we need to be transformed in His Presence and leave different than when we came to church. I am not saying these are the theological implications of this passage, I am simply sharing some of the value I receive in my spirit from seeing these kinds of *types* (or illustrations, if you prefer).

This passage and others, portraying physical *offerings*, have helped me immensely over the years to maintain a high level of reverence both in private worship and in public worship gatherings. As I enter a *church* gathering, I must remove all preoccupation with the world, and prepare my heart for helping the congregation come into His Holy Presence together.

I am aghast sometimes at the casual manner by which we often enter His place of corporate worship. He has done SO much for us; we dare not take for granted our spiritual blessings due SOLELY to His degrading sacrifice for our sins. Think of Ezekiel 46 next time you enter 'church' and prayerfully ponder: *Whom* you are actually gathering for (not for yourself)?

Bear with me for one more. I love the many visuals from the 'tabernacle' God designed and established for His people Israel, as they passed through the wilderness toward the Promised Land. Moses was given precise directions for its construction. One example is the covering of the tabernacle, under which sacrifices for sin were offered, and the Holy of holies was housed. Exodus 26:14 details, "And you shall make a covering for the tent of ram's skins dyed red, and a covering of porpoise skins above". I have been awed at the choice of materials and colors for this covering over which God touched humanity so deeply.

First, observe the 'hidden' covering. It was to be of ram's skins. The ram is a symbol of Christ in the Old Testament. We see a great picture of this in the story of Abraham when he was asked to take his son Isaac up the mountain and sacrifice him. Of course the Lord taught him his lesson, and provided another sacrifice. Here is what is recounted:

"Do not stretch out your hand against the lad, and do nothing to him; for now I know that you fear God, since you have not withheld your son, your only son, from Me. Then Abraham raised his eyes and looked, and behold, behind him a ram caught in the thicket by his horns; and Abraham went and took the ram, and offered him up for a burnt offering in the place of his son."
Genesis 22:12-13

This covering was to be dyed red. Red, of course, symbolizes Christ's blood, shed on the cross for the forgiveness of our sins. It brings tears to my eyes! Only from the inside of the tent, where we meet personally and intimately with the Godhead, can Christ's blood red sacrifice be observed.

On the outside is a very different sight! The crowd from afar only saw the tent of meeting as a dull grey color of porpoise skins. The worldly, the very ordinary, covered over the precious, holy sanctuary. What a portrayal of how different the world views the Christian faith from what we know as worth expending each breath for, and even worth dying for!

I trust these few smatterings of Old Testament images will likewise inspire you to dig deeper into the pages of His word, and allow God to disclose some of the depths of Christ's glory to your own heart and soul!

TRINITY

*I absolutely love
the way God made
so many things
in threes!*

TRINITY
GOD WORKS IN THREES!

Category	FATHER	SON	HOLY SPIRIT
Godhead	Father	Son	Spirit
Jesus	way	truth	life
Man in God's Image	soul	body	spirit
Man's Operations	will	mind	emotions
Enemies	world	flesh	devil
Man's sinful activities	lust of the eyes	lust of the flesh	boastful pride of life
Primary colors	green	red	blue
Music	melody	harmony	rhythm
Belief aids	love	faith	hope

I absolutely love the way God made so many things in threes! They not only demonstrate His wonderfully creative, yet orderly design, but illustrate precious truths for us to grasp!

Godhead

God Himself is a Trinity of Father, Son and Holy Spirit. He is One, yet three Persons, each having distinct roles within the Godhead. The Father laid out the plan, so to speak, 'creating the heavens and the earth' (Genesis 1:1), gave 'all things into the hands' (John 13:3) of His Son to implement for our redemption from sin, and sent the Spirit to guide us in responding to our salvation, by walking with Him (John 14:16-17; Galatians 5:16).

He is a Triune God, and we are made "in His image" and 'according to His likeness' (Genesis 1:26-27). It is within His creative will to surround us with things that speak of His Triune Nature. Since His 'ways and thoughts are so far above ours' (Isaiah 55:9), He places 'pictures' in creation to give us visual aids for understanding Him.

Jesus

In responding to human frailty even among His disciples, Jesus declared, "I am the way, and the truth, and the life; no one comes to the Father, but through Me" (John 14:6). This beautiful trinity of truths describing our Saviour, fills out so much of our understanding of His purpose for coming to earth. Many religions try to 'point the way' to God. Jesus came not just to point the way, but to 'provide the way' to be restored into God's Holy and eternal Presence. He expresses it as a 'narrow way' and adds that "few are those who find it" (Matthew 7:14). How vital it is, then, to receive His prescribed path for salvation, restoration and eternal life.

Many will tell you their opinion of what is 'true' to their meagre human minds, but as God is the essence of Love, so Jesus is the embodiment of *truth*. When John introduced Jesus in his gospel, He asserted, "For the Law was given through Moses; grace and truth were realized through Jesus Christ" (John 1:17). Coming to have faith in Jesus for salvation requires us to believe His teachings are true.

Rounding out this glorious trinity, He is also the *life*. He declared, Himself, "I came that they might have life, and might have *it* abundantly" (John 10:10). *Abundant* life can be realized right now, through the Spirit He sent to enliven our hearts and fill us with passion for Him!

John framed the bookends of His gospel with this conclusion:

"Many other signs therefore Jesus also performed in the presence of the disciples, which are not written in this book; but these have been written that you may believe that Jesus is the Christ, the Son of God; and that believing you may have life in His name." John 20:30-31

The 'life' spoken of here is not just on this side of the grave, but a true life that extends through all eternity. Peter explained it this way,

"for you have been born again not of seed which is perishable but imperishable, that is, through the living and abiding word of God." 1 Peter 1:23

My life has been immeasurably blessed by having Jesus as my Way, my Truth, and the best love of my Life!

Man

For centuries now biblical scholars have argued over whether the soul and spirit of a man are one and the same, or separate entities. I don't understand all the theological 'fuss' over this. It is simply in God's nature to create primary things in threes. So why argue with God? Again, this is not a theological work, but it makes so much sense to me that an orderly and consistent God would separate our 'likeness' to Him in three parts: soul, body and spirit. The core of the *soul* associates best with God, the *body* with Christ, and, of course, the *spirit* with His Spirit.

Our soul, the center of our being could not find a better 'fit' than with God Himself. When God created man, He "breathed into his nostrils the breath of life; and man became a living being [soul]" (Genesis 2:7b). One of King David's prayers included, "Make glad the soul of Thy servant, for to Thee, O Lord, I lift up my soul" (Psalm 86:4). Our soul is what our Creator God draws to Himself for salvation and redemption.

Jesus came in the *flesh*, took on *bodily* human form (fully God/fully man) and dwelt among us for a season, as the apex of human history. He 'sympathises with our weaknesses, was tempted in all things as we are, yet without personal sin' (Hebrews 4:15). How marvellous to have such a tangible part of the Godhead to relate with in our own body of flesh. This human expression of God demonstrates His unconditional love for us, by providing the kind of Saviour our severely limited minds can sufficiently comprehend to receive salvation from!

And of course, our *spirit* interacts with His Holy Spirit so sweetly and intimately. "The Spirit Himself bears witness with our spirit that we are children of God" (Romans 8:16). Just as the Spirit enlivens us, so our own spirit animates our life to "walk in newness of life" (Romans 6:4b). Our spirit is to submit to His Spirit, for the contrary 'grieves His Spirit' (Ephesians 4:30) and leads to our spiritual demise.

Soul

Even our *soul*, by itself, has been described as containing and operating by three aspects: mind, will and emotions. To me, these marvellously correspond with the *will* of God (Matthew 26:42b), the *mind* of Christ (1 Corinthians 2:16) and the energizing *power* of the Spirit (2 Corinthians 3:18; Romans 15:13).

When we surrender our *will* to God, He directs our pathway through life. Because He created us, counts every hair on our head, knows our beginning to our end, and loves us utterly and unconditionally, He is absolutely the best Person to direct our ways through this glorious life experience He has given us.

Every day, hour or moment given to Him to order and direct creates the best life we could possibly live. I tell people all the time that there is no better life to be lived than to have a 'God Story' every day. "Guess what God did today!" "Let me tell you how God worked through me this morning!" "I've just got to tell you what God did for me last night!" What a privilege to walk alongside our Creator and be connected with Him, for the precious people in this world!

But how do we know His will? How do we even get connected somehow with His 'narrow path' (Matthew 7:14) for us, let alone remain in that state over any length of time? Surrendering our will to Him opens the door, but how do we 'know' what and how He wants us to surrender? Well that is the beauty of 'threes'. Since we are made in His image and He has three parts to His whole, we also have two more parts to our soul that join with Him in a process of joyful surrender, making this connectedness a solid reality.

Incorporating the other two parts of the Trinity unlock the secret of knowing His will for us! The Bible says clearly that we can have the *mind* of Christ. The second part of the Trinity, Jesus Christ, wants to be the Lord of our lives, not just our Saviour, but our Lord. He is the part of the Godhead who is like the Head of our body, which directs all that our physical body responds to.

To me this means our thoughts can be directed by Jesus, in cooperation with His Word, the Bible, which was crafted by His mind and written for our instruction. As I try and remain surrendered to what God has in store for my day, Jesus and His Word direct the 'way' in which I execute my day. Surrendering to His instructions will improve my character, morality, manner and circumstances, as Jesus is given more and more control of my being.

The Third Person of the Trinity, the Holy Spirit of God fulfills the completion of the process by guiding our *emotions,* and filling us with passion for God's will. Now let me add here that emotions are given by God as *indicator lights*, revealing both good and bad things going on inside of us. They are not meant to be *tools* for us to wield.

The Holy Spirit, as the animated part of the Godhead stirs up the positive emotions of our being to give us the enjoyment of surrendering to God. Positive emotions 'indicate' great things happening internally. The joy unspeakable, peace that passes all understanding and loving passion for walking out the daily assignments of God's Kingdom come through submitting our human spirit to His Holy Spirit.

Negative emotions are meant to 'indicate' warnings to pay attention to, and repair, not tools for us to wield. When negative emotions well up inside us, we must let the Spirit guide us as to why they have been stirred up, and to provide a better way forward than lashing out with them, or stuffing them, both to our detriment.

For instance, you are sitting in a chair in the yard, and your child keeps playing on a large mound of earth, located beside a large hole in the ground. Your repeated requests to stay off the mound are ignored. You feel agitation welling up inside you, leading to anger.

At this point you can wield the anger, grab your child's arm, yank them off the mound and spank them, while yelling at them to listen to you! The harder (biblical culture) path is taking the time to evaluate why the anger is within you, before the Lord. Yes, the child needs instruction, but your anger is not meant to be the tool for the lesson. So instead, God reveals a better path.

You go to the child, get down to their level, gaining their full attention, and tell them how much you love them. You explain how terrible it would be if they fell into that hole and got hurt. Then you take them to the 'safe' side of the mound and show them the boundaries they *can* play in, perhaps even taking a bit of time to join them in their fun.

I mention this here, because negative emotions can destroy *love* and *self-esteem*, whereas positive emotions can bring life and light.

Regarding anger, the Lord is a great model. Psalm 145:8 says, "The Lord is gracious and merciful; slow to anger and great in lovingkindness. Proverbs 14:29 teaches, "He who is slow to anger has great understanding, but he who is quick-tempered exalts folly."

The role of the Holy Spirit here is to guide us in the midst of negative emotions 'into all truth' (John 16:13a), so we can return to positive emotions and fully enjoy the will of God through our lives.

When it comes to our will, mind and emotions, many confidently proclaim what the will of God is for their lives. Sadly, much of that is, in fact, merely circumstantial, or fleshly desires seeking God's blessings upon them. It is by His power that we actually set aside the 'desires of the flesh', the only means of cooperating with the will of God and restoring the mind of Christ. And it is in 'walking by the Spirit' that the will of God unfolds before us. It is more realized than known ahead of time. It is 'by faith' and not by sight.

So the Trinity of soul, when surrendered to the Father, Son and Holy Spirit, creates in and through us the greatest core of meaning and purpose that our lives could possibly experience. May each of you reading this find the narrow path I am speaking of!

Enemies

God labels three external foes we must guard against lest we become completely and deceptively enveloped by our surrounding cultural norms and values; the *world*, the *flesh* and the *devil*.

The *world* is the culture surrounding us; the honking horns, the flashing ads, the tainted values, all vying for our conformity. Romans 12:2 implores,

> *"do not be conformed to this world, but be transformed by the renewing of your mind, that you may prove what the will of God is, that which is good and acceptable and perfect."*

The *flesh* is our own tainted human desire to succumb and conform to those temporal ways of the world. Galatians 5:16 advises, "walk by the Spirit, and you will not carry out the desire of the flesh." In the next chapter we are also warned,

"For the one who sows to his own flesh shall from the flesh reap corruption, but the one who sows to the Spirit shall from the Spirit reap eternal life."   *Galatians 6:8*

And the *devil*, the enemy of our soul, loudly tempts us all toward destructive thoughts, attitudes and actions. As the "accuser of our brethren" (Revelation 12:10), he attempts to demoralize our faith, and render our message ineffective. 2 Timothy 2:24-26 explains,

"And the Lord's bond-servant must not be quarrelsome, but be kind to all, able to teach, patient when wronged, with gentleness correcting those who are in opposition, if perhaps God may grant them repentance leading to the knowledge of the truth, and they may come to their senses and escape from the snare of the devil, having been held captive by him to do his will."

Lusts

This leads us to a trinity of 'internal' enemies of God we need to have an imperative awareness of, and a keen aversion to. 1 John 2:16 labels these enemies, "the lust of the flesh and the lust of the eyes and the boastful pride of life." These three stand against the Trinity, our fortress of protection from these brazen foes.

The *eyes* correspond with the Father, who sees all and knows all. Our *eyes*, the way we see and respond to the *world* He created, either cooperates with His purposes or 'lusts' after the things the world sets before our eyes to desire. 2 Peter 2:14 defines unrighteous souls as "having eyes full of adultery". The Word speaks much about the 'eyes', either as seeing God clearly or as blind in the darkness of opposing behaviour. Matthew 6:22-23 explains the magnitude of this problem;

"The lamp of the body is the eye; if therefore your eye is clear, your whole body will be full of light. But if your eye is bad, your whole body will be full of darkness."

It goes on to warn,

"If therefore the light that is in you is darkness, how great is the darkness!"   (Verse 23b)

It reminds me of Jesus speaking about those in the church whose deeds are 'lukewarm', and thus are 'spit out of His mouth', and in the worse condition possible (Revelation 3:15-16). Matthew 7:5 recommends, "first take the log out of your own eye, and then you will see clearly to take the speck out of your brother's eye." And in Matthew 18:9, stressing the importance of denying visual lusts, we read,

"And if your eye causes you to stumble, pluck it out, and throw it from you. It is better for you to enter life with one eye, than having two eyes to be cast into the fiery hell."

Of course the preferred action is to keep "fixing our eyes on Jesus, the author and perfecter of faith" (Hebrews 12:2).

And so the *lust of the eyes*, longing for and looking at the wrong sources for fulfillment, will always lead to a degrading spiral toward darkness. The internet has become a devastating source for the eyes, especially since the viewer often falsely believes no one will know what is being done in the darkness. But Jesus declared, "there is nothing covered up that will not be revealed" (Luke 12:2a).

When it comes to the *flesh*, it connects with Jesus, who came to earth 'in the flesh' (John 1:14). He 'sympathizes with our weaknesses' and was 'tempted in all things like us, yet without sin' (Hebrews 4:15). Having said that, we know He allows no place for carrying out the *lusts* of our flesh, with their sinful desires and passions. Rather, He is our Model for denying the fleshly 'self', and walking by the Spirit.

Both the cultures of the world and our own human frailties drive us toward the consumption of fleshly lusts. Only by conforming daily to the ways of Christ can we be protected from them. Happily, we are assured that

"No temptation has overtaken you but such as is common to man; and God is faithful, who will not allow you to be tempted beyond what you are able, but with the temptation will provide the way of escape also, that you may be able to endure it."
1 Corinthians 10:13

So how does this play out in real life? Well, for example, there are a lot of beautiful young island girls down here in Roatan, many of whom brazenly display their wares. When I see this on the street, I am tempted to gaze for a while, or linger in my thoughts about them... or... thank God for giving me such a love for Him that I choose, by His strength, to turn my attention elsewhere and think on healthier things. The Apostle Paul portrayed his own personal struggle throughout Romans 7, and then decried, "Wretched man that I am! Who will set me free from the body of this death?" (Verse 24) He then responded, "Thanks be to God through Jesus Christ our Lord!" (Verse 25a)

My love for Jesus has truly diminished my 'lust' for many things, like sporty cars, a large house, showy possessions, a grand reputation, the adoration of friends, etc. Once He actually becomes the love of your life and the source of your fulfillment, other things will pale by comparison. Yes, the temptations remain and are very real, but the ability to resist them far exceeds the desire, never wanting to disappoint our Lord. Paul stated categorically, "I buffet my body and make it my slave, lest possibly, after I have preached to others, I myself should be disqualified" (1 Corinthians 9:27). Similarly, this is my commitment to the Lord!

The third enemy of our soul is *the boastful pride of life*, rearing its ugly head over against the Spirit. Have you noticed in Galatians 5:22 that 'pride' is not a fruit of the Spirit? Verses 25-26a follow with, "If we live by the Spirit, let us also walk by the Spirit. Let us not become boastful". Galatians 6 proceeds with a series of ways to walk humbly instead. Incidentally, walking humbly is one of another set of *three*s laid out in Micah 6:8 as commendable: "to do justice, to love kindness and to walk humbly with your God".

1 Peter 5:5-6 admonishes,

> *"all of you, clothe yourselves with humility toward one another,*
> *for God is OPPOSED TO THE PROUD, BUT GIVES GRACE to the*
> *humble. Humble yourselves, therefore, under the mighty hand*
> *of God, that He may exalt you at the proper time."*

Herein lays the problem. We are not to exalt ourselves. Applause for our 'successes' is up to God, and others, to bestow.

But sin is deceitful above all else and creeps in so subtly. We make comments like, 'Guess what I did for the Lord today!', or 'We had our largest attendance last Sunday!' or 'I don't go to that store anymore, they don't provide the service quality I am used to!' These all sound strangely like the arrogantly praying Pharisee in Luke 18:11-14;

> *"God, I thank Thee that I am not like other people: swindlers,*
> *unjust, adulterers, or even like this tax collector. 'I fast twice a*

week; I pay tithes of all that I get.' But the tax collector... was beating his breast, saying: 'God, be merciful to me, the sinner!' "I tell you, this man went down to his house justified rather than the other; for everyone who exalts himself shall be humbled, but he who humbles himself shall be exalted."

Jesus summarized all of this by declaring, "But the greatest among you shall be your servant" (Matthew 23:11).

The *boastful pride of life* is full of 'I' and 'me', and so many other self-exaltations, but the Spirit is actually the One who empowers, and therefore deserves all the credit and praise. My advice is to humbly redirect any praise from others to the Lord. Keep your finger pointing to Him and not to your own chest. The admonition is clear: beware the slippery slope of succumbing to the 'lust of the eyes, lust of the flesh and/or the boastful pride of life'. Instead, keep yourself firmly planted within the fortress of protection by the Father, Son and Holy Spirit.

Colors

I love colors! How dull this world would be without azure skies, turquoise seas, vibrant green foliage and countless other scenes of multi-colored splendour! But isn't it amazing that all of this beauty stems from an endless mixing of just three primary colors: *red, green* and *blue*. What further glorious symbols of our Triune God! Green wonderfully matches with God Himself. Did you know that *green* is the only color in the entire spectrum of the rainbow of colors that the human eye does not need to adjust to? Imagine that. The human eye was created by God to view green alone completely naturally, as we were always intended to see Him, prior to the fall of mankind into the devastating consequences of sin. Remember how Adam and Eve first hid from the face of God, afraid to see Him, fearing His displeasure for the first time.

But now, how utterly grateful we are for the *red* redeeming blood of Christ, shed to restore our fellowship with God. Yes, red has come to symbolize the blood of Christ, graciously opening the way back to the Father! Christ is the visible means to refocus our gaze back on God; "the exact representation of His Nature" (Hebrews 1:3). How stupendous to realise the foresight of God, using red as a primary symbol of Christ long before His arrival on our planet (e.g. Exodus 26:14)! How comforting to observe God's pre-ordained plan come to fruition through His Son, and to know He has complete charge over the rest of human history ahead!

And *blue*... ah, lest we forget the third primary color. This symbol of water is inseparably linked to His Spirit. In Genesis 1:2 we are informed, "The Spirit of God was moving over the surface of the waters." John declared in Matthew 3:11, "I baptize you with water for repentance, but He who is coming after me is mightier than I... He will baptize you with the Holy Spirit". And I find it fascinating that in Luke 11:24 the 'unclean spirits' are associated with 'waterless places'.

Clearly again, a balanced view of, and intimate focus on the Trinity should produce in our lives similar variety and splendour to the myriad of colors around us, in this world He has given us 'to enjoy' (1 Timothy 6:17b).

Music

Here is yet another spectacular tri-part symbol, He had blessed us with 'to enjoy'. We all love and favour certain types of music, performers, bands, orchestrations. But regardless of our varying preferences, music certainly enhances all of our lives, stirs us up, and gets us going!

Music has held a significant role in my life since my first piano lesson at the ripe old age of four. I have played piano, guitar, bass, clarinet, saxophone, oboe and even dabbled with flute and fiddle. With the onset and miniaturization of technology, most people now have ready access to music right in their pockets!

But have you ever considered how music is linked with the Trinity? Music is essentially made up of three distinct parts: *melody, harmony* and *rhythm*, yet emerges as one single presentation. The *melody* is God's wooing Voice to the world He has set in motion. He speaks the melody through His people, through life's circumstances, even through nature itself. Romans 1:20 declares,

> *"For since the creation of the world His invisible attributes, His eternal power and divine nature, have been clearly seen, being understood through what has been made,"*

It flows to both the heights and the depths of the octaves of life and clearly declares His song to each precious soul. It stands alone as sufficient to carry us through our entire journey.

But now imagine that same melody with the glorious enhancement of a perfectly accompanying *harmony*, helping to fill out the song's flow with a bright and harmonious Voice! Jesus is the perfect enhancement of the Voice of God, always in harmony, never in dissonance. Hebrews 1:3 declares, "He is the radiance of His [God's] glory and the exact representation of His nature". He faithfully declared, "I do nothing on My own initiative, but I speak these things as the Father taught Me... for I always do the things that are pleasing to Him" (John 8:28-29b).

Oh what glorious moments when we are used, under Christ, to be the harmony to God's melody of activity in this world. But oh the dissonance we create, when we rebelliously disobey and thus 'grieve the Spirit' (Ephesians 4:30), by speaking or behaving in a different key than the melody. How redeeming it is that His melody cannot be thwarted. Praise Him for the Voice of truth that will 'never pass away'! (Mark 13:31)

And praise Him for His Spirit, the *rhythm* of His song, the beat to His music, the One who animates the melody and harmony, and launches it into dance! How I love the kind of music that gets your toe tapping, that makes you try to break dance on the sidewalk, that brightens your darkness and sets you on fire with praise! How much better is God's song and Jesus' perfect harmony when activated and empowered by the Spirit of truth beating through your life. The entire Trinity is meant to produce a symphony of glorious sound from your life, impacting a needy world for His Kingdom glory!

Love

After an entire chapter outlining the unsurpassing value of love as the motivating factor for all virtuous spiritual ventures, 1 Corinthians 13 concludes with this statement, "But now abide faith, hope, love, these three; but the greatest of these is love" (verse 13). Here again, even in a chapter about one topic, *love* (which corresponds with God), a trinity of elements are enjoined as abiding through all generations.

1 John 4:16b asserts, "God is love, and the one who abides in love abides in God, and God abides in him." What a tremendous truth to internalize. God is not just a loving guy, as many by their actions try to reduce Him to. God IS love. He is the embodiment and source of every loving action. His essence is love. Since God is eternal, it follows that His loving Character abides forever.

Yet even given this enormous fact, detailed throughout the great love chapter, God intentionally includes the other two parts of the Trinity in the process.

Faith perfectly matches with Jesus! For example, there is a passage in Galatians 2 which reads,

> "knowing that a man is not justified by the works of the law
> but through faith in Christ Jesus, even we have believed in Christ

Jesus, that we may be justified by faith in Christ, and not by the works of the Law."   *Verse 16*

Faith in Jesus is the essential foundation of our beliefs, and He is rightly called the "CORNER *stone*" of our faith (Acts 4:11-12). Christ is also eternal, so our faith in Him can never be undermined by His destruction.

And *hope* wonderfully aligns with the Holy Spirit. It is the more emotional, animated element! Much of 'hope' in this world is no more than wishful thinking. "I hope it doesn't rain today". "Well, I hope I get that promotion soon." But hope in God, who is eternal, is a hope with certainty, with guaranteed results! When people ask me how I am doing, I often reply, "Better than yesterday, because I am one day closer to heaven!"

Hope in God enlivens the soul and brings deep inner joy, even in the midst of great suffering and human loss. Hope in God keeps us going through the darkest of days, and resets our footing back to solid ground. Romans 5:1-6 outlines a number of things we receive through tribulations, one of them being *hope*. Verse 5 offers, "and hope does not disappoint, because the love of God has been poured out within our hearts through the Holy Spirit who was given to us."

So even in a passage about God's attribute of love (1 Corinthians 13), He refuses to stand alone, but defers to the Trinity of His Godhead. Such loyalty should be a model for us to follow in sticking with Him and our *brethren* in Christ throughout our lives.

WORLD

ORIGINS

Knowing the genius of God
and His awesome propensity
toward order from beginning to end,
I believe the Garden of Eden was
where Jerusalem is located today!

I have no opposition to science.
In fact, my definition of
noble scientific pursuit is simply,
"Figuring out how God does stuff".

I believe in a factual universal flood as outlined in the biblical book of Genesis. It best accounts for the details of earth's progression from that time forward. One of the leading arguments against this is the use of 'carbon dating', a process purported to date things in the millions of years old. As carbon dating has proven unreliable, this prime argument has diminished.

We will never have all the details, because God's purpose in crafting the Scriptures was never to provide them all. But if you simply take a globe (like the one we all got distracted with during a boring science class) and look at the entire earth, you will see that by figuratively removing all the large bodies of water, every piece of land fits neatly together, by compressing the land masses to form a smaller ball. To me this indicates that prior to the flood, the world had a much different configuration and appearance. We do know that a mist used to rise from the earth, an indication that the relationship of water to the earth was significantly different.

Now here is the coolest part. By examining the globe carefully, you can observe the geological results of a great body of water 'emerging' from within the earth, out of the Dead Sea (earth's lowest elevation, by the way).

We know that a river flowed out of the Garden of Eden and divided into four (Pishon, Gihon, Tigris and Euphrates – Genesis 2:11-14). Scholars use the current position of the Euphrates to determine where Eden might have been. But if the earth was configured differently before the 'flood', then the current Euphrates cannot be used as a guide for pinpointing the location of Eden.

Here is my theory. Knowing the genius of God and His awesome propensity toward order from beginning to end, I believe the Garden of Eden was where Jerusalem is located today! Wouldn't that be just like God? And as the Bible describes the flood, waters came out of the earth, as well as from the heavens. So it would make sense that those waters came up through what is now the Dead Sea, 'coincidently', in close proximity to Jerusalem itself!

Notice on the globe how the current rivers, furrows and seas extend outward from the Dead Sea, as though this is where they settled when the bulk of the flood waters receded to the ocean cavities. The cavities would likely have been created for them by the weight of the heaven-sent flood waters coupled with the exodus of the waters from inside the earth.

Now let's consider the part of the waters that came from above. You need to realize that if the world indeed was rotating in some form, which it must have been to have human habitation cling to it with gravitational force, then the flood waters would not have fallen as rain the world over. In the northern and southern regions it would have fallen as snow or sleet and accumulated as ice... and voila, an instant 'ice age', as many describe it. So if the flood created an instant body of ice over two thirds of the earth, then what we have been observing since that time, has been the ever so gradual recession of that ice in polar directions, due to a now warmer earth.

Many scientists reject this possibility, because they start with the premise that no universal flood occurred. Now I have no opposition to science. In fact, my definition of noble scientific pursuit is simply, "Figuring out how God does stuff". My beef with much of the scientific community is the use of incorrect premises as starting points for their purported theories. Scientists who include the flood as a valid proposition, are uncovering a host of better explanations for the texture and progression of the surface of the earth.

DEMOCRACY

I contend that the only
system of governance that 'works'
is an autocratic system,
but God needs to be the Head of it.
This is the heart of a biblical culture!

True democracy is forged for the good of all its equally valued citizens. It is properly based upon *cooperation*, not *competition*. Being other-centered is a necessary ingredient, or the system denigrates over time. As a community cooperates for the good of all, ownership is achieved and participation cultivated.

Once competition sets in, adversity comes into play, winning takes precedence, and 'success' is derived at the *expense* of the other.

I contend that due to greed, and other sinful tendencies in each of us, the only system of governance that 'works' is an autocratic system; but God needs to be the Head of it. This is the heart of a biblical culture!

The American vision of democracy began with the desired freedom to worship God, and to construct laws for the good of each community, based upon equality, rather than being abusively ruled by an elite monarchy. Along this noble path, however, it somehow became acceptable to kill off the existing population, to make room for this democracy. It became acceptable to enlist slaves, young children and the oppressed poor to serve the accumulation of wealth.

It has since devolved into a self-seeking individualistic quest for personal wealth without constraint, even at the expense of other cultures. If you are 'smart enough' you can devise a product, convince millions they 'need' it, get low wage workers (in impoverished cultures) to produce it and make millions of dollars for yourself. The only 'democratic' part left of this concept, is that no one will tell you not to do it!

Now picture a company where the boss makes the same wage as the workers. Everyone shares equally the blessings of a profitable business, without overcharging the valued customers, offering them the lowest possible price points over time. This kind of venture is considered 'foolish' to the world, but honourable in the eyes of God.

As China emerges as the dominant power on earth, they are being labeled the 'BLING DYNASTY'. The new American style of 'democracy' has taught them well, and their new 'religion' is the worship of money. The Chinese elite now have an insatiable appetite for luxury that will not be quenched! Of course, this is just another step toward the end of our planet as we know it, with God permitting this demise until the moment of the return of His Son, Christ Jesus. He will eventually come to judge each person for either eternal salvation or eternal separation, and to finally 'govern' a new heaven and earth!

ORGANIZATIONS

If God determines change
to a group or entity,
we will only be fighting against Him
if we stubbornly keep it going 'at all costs'.
There is a mysterious balance here
between perseverance and disobedience.

Let me share a few brief thoughts about the larger institutions we organize. There are numerous examples of God raising up and removing nations and peoples for His greater purposes in our unfolding human history. In Deuteronomy 7:1, for example, He 'clears away many nations' for Israel to repossess the land given them to dwell. In fact, Israel had seasons of time in the holy land, seasons in exile from it, seasons of prosperity and seasons of famine. As Ecclesiastes 3:1-8 outlines, 'there is an appointed time for all things under the sun'.

If we apply this truth to our generation, it follows that whatever nation, organization, company or church congregation we may start or participate in, will at some point terminate.

I am making this point here to help you look through a better lens at your workplace, your church building, your denomination or your extra-curricular group. All these organizations in some fashion or manner are ultimately used by God in their 'season' to fulfil His greater purposes. Acts 17:24 reads,

> *"The God who made the world and all things in it, since He is*
> *Lord of heaven and earth, does not dwell in temples made with*
> *hands; neither is He served by human hands, as though He*

needed anything, since He Himself gives to all life and breath and all things; and He made from one, every nation of mankind to live on all the face of the earth, having determined their appointed times and the boundaries of their habitation,"

So our job is not to keep an organization going indefinitely. Our expectation should not be to remain in the same job through the course of our entire career. I want you to maintain a healthy and accurate perspective here. We are not 'entitled' to have things stay 'the way they've always been', nor is 'we've always done it this way' a proper posture. If God determines change to a group or entity, we will only be fighting against Him if we stubbornly keep it going 'at all costs'. There is a mysterious balance here between perseverance and disobedience.

For instance, you have worked for a company for 15 years and then they downsize and you are one of the ones laid off. Now you have two options, depending on whether you believe in the sovereignty of God or not. You can rail at the company for abandoning you after so many years of faithful service, OR you can thank them for providing for your family for 15 years, and thank God that He will continue to provide, according to His will, for the days ahead. The reality is that companies do not last forever. They have a season of productivity and you are extended a blessing for the season you receive from it.

Let me give you another example. There may come a time when your church congregation ceases to serve the community effectively. God knows this, and plans something new and more effective. However, your group determines to do everything 'in its power' to keep it going; fundraisers, outreach to gain more members which will supply more funds. In a circumstance of this nature, you are, in fact, fighting against God Himself, who is ending the season of one congregation to rise up another. We do not 'deserve' to have everything we want to last a lifetime. We are promised 'food and covering' (1 Timothy 6:8), like the sparrows are afforded, and everything else is a blessing. 1 Thessalonians 5:18 lends perspective with "in everything give thanks".

I knew of one Bible College who believed they must 'always' have a new development project in order to keep large donors giving to them, and not another entity. Their stated strategy was: 'if we are not growing, we are declining'. While this may have seemed a 'wise' philosophy from a purely business standpoint, the better lens is a heart in tune with God's leading, for BOTH the developing and the decline of an organization. I believe organizations and churches alike should have godly plans leading to termination, and not simply plans for growth. Growth is not meant to proceed forever, and decline does not need to be 'messy', in God's economy.

If God seems to be closing down a work, then it should be done joyfully and gracefully, with great anticipation of where He is leading next. It was Daniel who said,

> "Let the name of God be blessed forever and ever, for wisdom and power belong to Him. And it is He who changes the times and the epochs; He removes kings and establishes kings; He gives wisdom to wise men, and knowledge to men of understanding."
> Daniel 2:20

Only through God's eternal lens can we remain content with His leading, in any direction He chooses, both for our cherished institutions and for our nations.

DESTINY

His plan for human history
continues to unfold
according to His authoritative power.
Our allegiance must be placed in His will,
not the self-seeking desires
of any particular country
we reside in.

Governments, believe it or not, are instituted by God, and their leaders are appointed by Him. Romans 13:1-2 remind us,

"Let every person be in subjection to the governing authorities. For there is no authority except from God, and those which exist are established by God. Therefore he who resists authority has opposed the ordinance of God; and they who have opposed will receive condemnation upon themselves."

Now there are times when as Peter and the other apostles declared. "We must obey God rather than men" (Acts 5:29), but this was an instance where an 'angel of the Lord' specifically said to "speak to the people" (verse 20) and the human authorities told them to be silent (verse 28). The point I am making here, though, is that it is ultimately God who sets leaders in place, both good and evil. He is ever in charge of human history. His plan for human history continues to unfold according to His authoritative power. Our allegiance must be placed in His will, not the self-seeking desires of any particular country we reside in.

So those who would live a biblical culture must understand and maintain a sweeping view of God's activity through human history, and not risk the deceit of media induced indoctrination as to current local events and what we should think about them, how we should respond to them and who we are pushed to vote for.

While God loves all of mankind and shows no partiality (i.e. no preference for one person over another), He set Israel uniquely upon this planet as His representative people. In this 'church age' Israel has been 'hardened', so the Gentile church has opportunity to be 'grafted' into their family tree (see Romans 11:25-31). But as this age draws to a close, our world focus must remain centered upon Israel, and not the culture we happen to live in. Our destiny is for this world to end, and for a new heaven and a new earth to be formed (see 2 Peter 3:13).

Since I grew up in North America, let me share a few thoughts from that perspective. First let's consider Canada. In my lifetime growing up there, I believe Pierre Trudeau, more than any other Prime Minister of my time, contributed to the destruction of the moral fabric of the country. His legacy, the "Canadian *Charter of Rights and Freedoms*", gave minority groups *greater* protections than the rights of the majority. This tipped the scale toward a growing culture of 'everyone doing what is right in their own eyes' (Judges 21:25), and Canadian culture has been further secularizing ever since.

Mr. Trudeau was not supportive of Israel, and even sidled up to the Palestinians later in office. However, subsequent leaders have offered strong protection for Israel, and I believe this, more than anything else, contributes to the ongoing benefits of life in Canada. But those days are drawing to a close. Now that his son Justin holds the office of Prime Minister, we will see how God uses him in His unfolding plan.

In the United States, support for Israel has been powerful and protective since the Second World War. Yet here is where I sense a major shift in relation to Israel and our closing in on the final destiny of our darkening world. I contend that President George W. Bush's actions removed *respect* for the United States in the Middle East. He artificially created a category of people labelled 'terrorists', and set the 'civilized' world on a new course to kill them all. He should have known from Hitler that you can't begin to eradicate an entire group of people without others rising up to kill you back! In effect, He has fostered a whole new generation of groups bent on the destruction of America, in retaliation and revenge.

President Obama's activities have now removed the *fear* of America in the Middle East. His growing removal of support for Israel after 70 years of American protection, is contributing toward their vulnerability to the nations around them. His legacy will be to have caused the circumstances for a nuclear arsenal to be amassed for the sole purpose of eradicating Israel.

But I hold that this is all happening by God's authority and design. As the world draws to a close, how else could nations rise up against Israel, unless those who have been protecting it all these years are diminished in their capacity or willingness to do so? The Bible further speaks of God never destroying the world again with a flood of water, but refers instead to the heavens and the earth passing away from 'intense heat' (2 Peter 3:10). Zechariah predicted, "For I will gather all the nations against Jerusalem to battle" (14:2a). He goes on to detail,

"Now this will be the plague with which the Lord will strike all the peoples who have gone to war against Jerusalem; their flesh will rot while they stand on their feet, and their eyes will rot in their sockets, and their tongue will rot in their mouth."
Verse 12

Now I have no understanding of how it will all unfold, but this all sounds eerily 'nuclear' to me. And the reality of nuclear solutions has gripped the minds of those who are driven to wipe Israel off the face of the earth in these very days we live in.

It is my firm belief that in these days, the disciples of Jesus must more than ever relinquish prime allegiance to their country of origin, and pledge full allegiance to God and His representatives, Israel. When it comes to elections for your leaders, my commitment is to find out two things.

First, I want to know which candidate is most likely to be influenced by God. Second, I want to know which candidate most strongly stands with Israel and supports its protection. Given the extent of our drivenness to comfort, greed and self-centeredness, every candidate promises 'more jobs' and 'lower taxes'... blah, blah, blah. Don't be fooled by their speeches, or be deceived by the biases of news media.

God is doing universal things we catch only glimpses of, but as citizens of His Kingdom, I know when I come before the 'judgment seat' I want to be able to confidently say, "I stood with You and Your people Lord", not "I got a good tax break"!

DEATH

If He had chosen to simply
turn off the switch
of an ever healthy body,
we might never experience
the growing passion of
longing for heaven,
nor the anticipated joy of
experiencing freedom
from these fleeting vessels.

How ingenious of God to allow our bodies to disintegrate through to the end of our life. If He had chosen to simply turn off the switch of an ever healthy body we might never experience the growing passion of longing for heaven, nor the anticipated joy of experiencing freedom from these fleeting vessels. Whichever body parts start to fail first, in large part determines the manner and painfulness of our ending. But however it happens, barring accidental death, the longing of our soul to be released from this body of pain and frailness increases as we age.

In similar fashion the end of this earth as we know it seems to be following the same imagery and pattern as the human body. We are wearing out this planet, using up its resources, diminishing both food and water sources, polluting the skies and reaping the consequences of a dying planet. God declared that in the end times "most people's love will grow cold" (Matthew 24:12b), and we see the evidence of this worldwide as the nations get older and grumpier... we are not dying gracefully as a globe of inhabitants. Rather, we seem to want to kill each other off.

Of course, by God's higher design, everything revolves around Jerusalem and we need to read the signs, as the super powers shift to those who would support the nations desiring to eradicate Israel.

I have heard some people say they do not want to bring children into the world during these dreadful darkening days, but I choose to focus through the lens of God's activity and see it as a most fascinating era to be a part of. God's wish is for 'none to perish, but for all to come to eternal life' (2 Peter3:9b), yet the choice is ours individually. As each is given freewill, of course all will not choose to receive the saving Christ for forgiveness of sins and eternal life, but the ending of this earth marks so many joyous conclusions.

The concluding of this world by God will mark the end of sinful behaviour, the end of suffering in these bodily shells, the end of pain and sorrow, the end of darkness, of evil, of depression and the despair of poverty, the end of war and bitter hatred. There is no better time than in these darkening days to receive the living water Christ offers, so the empty longing of the human soul can be filled with the unequivocal love of God and the value of knowing and enjoying Him forever.

CONCLUSION

I want to thank whoever took the time to read through this personal compilation of thoughts on these various topics. For a period of about three months, during the spring of 2014 I was consistently waking up thinking about these things, and wanting to share them with the next generation. I started getting up early and just writing down whatever He brought to my mind. After this season, I left them in a file and went on with life. This summer (2015) I believe He prompted me to sort them together and produce this little book.

I have tried to be obedient in this endeavour, but I repeat; these are my thoughts. Some of them may also be His, and those are the ones you need to respond to.

Living a biblical culture is not for everyone. Some of you may think I am part of a 'cult'. Others may simply think it is too much to ask of a person, to devote their one entire life to God. A few of you are committed to following Jesus and are beginning to understand the value of choosing 'the narrow path' leading to real life! You are the ones this work is especially intended for.

My sincere hope and prayer is that everyone reading it will get 'something' out of it that inspires you to move closer to the Throne of God, both for your own best, and for the spiritual benefit of everyone around you. Let me end with a short poem/pathway to embrace:

LIVING A BIBLICAL CULTURE

Learn of His love intentionally

Receive His love joyfully

Fall in love with Him genuinely

Turn from your sins actually

Have faith in Him completely

Grow to love Him deeply

Get to know Him intimately

Become content with Him fully

Despise your sin utterly

Die to selfishness specifically

Devote yourself to others spiritually

Receive His promptings attentively

Serve Him responsively

Let His power work thoroughly

Long to be with Him eternally

Now the God of peace, who brought up from the dead the great Shepherd of the sheep through the blood of the eternal covenant, even Jesus our Lord, equip you in every good thing to do His will, working in us that which is pleasing in His sight, through Jesus Christ, to whom be the glory forever and ever. Amen.   Hebrews 13:20-21

NOTES

CAREER, p. 104

[1]Wisconsin Council on children & families: Brain Development and Early Learning [https://larrycuban.files.wordpress.com/2013/04/brain_dev_and_early_learning.pdf], paragraph 1.

CAREER, p. 105

[2]McClintock and Strong Encyclopaedia: Adult Age, cited in Louis Rushmore, *Marriage Ages in the Bible* [www.gospelgazette.com/gazette/2005/may/page20.htm], paragraph 3.

CLASSES, p. 115

[3]Payne, Ruby K.: A Framework for Understanding Poverty (aha! Process, Inc., 1996), p. 59.

GIFTS, p. 156

[4]Fortune, Don & Katie: Discover Your God-Given Gifts (Chosen Books, 1987), pp. 16-19.

ISSUES, p. 162

[5]Nee, Watchman: The Normal Christian Life, American Edition (Tyndale House Publishers, Inc., 1977).